D1586114

joy upon joy

CHARLES SPURGEON

WHITAKER
HOUSE

Publisher's Note: This new collection from Whitaker House is comprised of selections from Charles Spurgeon's complete original sermons. The resulting text has been edited for content and also updated for the modern reader. Words have been occasionally revised for clarity and readability.

All Scripture quotations are taken from the *King James Version Easy Read Bible*, KJVER®, © 2001, 2007, 2010, 2015 by Whitaker House. Used by permission. All rights reserved.

JOY UPON JOY:
An Advent Devotional

ISBN: 978-1-62911-958-8
eBook ISBN: 978-1-62911-959-5
Printed in the United States of America
© 2017 by Whitaker House

Whitaker House
1030 Hunt Valley Circle
New Kensington, PA 15068
www.whitakerhouse.com

No part of this book may be reproduced or transmitted in any form or by any means, electronic or mechanical—including photocopying, recording, or by any information storage and retrieval system—without permission in writing from the publisher. Please direct your inquiries to permissionseditor@whitakerhouse.com.

1 2 3 4 5 6 7 8 9 10 **W** 23 22 21 20 19 18 17

To

_____

From

_____

NOTE FROM THE PUBLISHER

Certainly Charles Spurgeon's masterful devotionals, *Morning and Evening* and *Faith's Checkbook*, do not need to be improved upon or replaced. Our purpose in crafting this Advent devotional from Spurgeon's writings is to bring to light treasures of his eloquence on the subject of waiting for and anticipating the incarnation by putting those writings into an accessible format. To that end, selections have been gleaned from a variety of his sermons and writings that bear out the glory of the Word become flesh in the first advent and the responsibility of the Christian to prepare for the second advent.

In his Christmas sermons, Spurgeon's theme was again and again the joy that believers can, and should, embody in response to the love of a God who, at the very beginning, did not cast aside the first Adam in disgust but rather promised to send a second Adam to redeem what man had broken. To that promise did centuries of men and women cling, and yet, as Spurgeon loved to remind his listeners, because Christ came to earth as Man, suffered, died, and was raised again, we have now an even greater promise—a second advent. Although we wait, we can wait with "joy upon joy" at what the incarnation accomplished.

With space to journal and reflect on the joy of our faith, may your seasonal devotions be touched by grace—not just of the pen of the "Prince of Preachers," Charles Spurgeon, but of the transformational grace conveyed by the "Prince of Peace," Himself.

—*Whitaker House*

WEEK 1

DAY 1
MORNING

"The consolation of Israel...."
—Luke 2:25

All the saints have waited for Jesus. Our mother Eve waited for the coming of Christ; when her first son was born, she said, *"I have gotten a man from the LORD"* (Genesis 4:1). True she was mistaken in what she said: it was Cain, and not Jesus. But by her mistake we see that she cherished the blessed hope. That Hebrew patriarch, who took his son, his only son, to offer him for a burnt offering, expected the Messiah, and well did he express his faith when he said, *"My son, God will provide Himself a lamb"* (Genesis 22:8). He who once had a stone for his pillow, the trees for his curtains, the heaven for his canopy, and the cold ground for his bed, expected the coming of Jesus, for he said on his deathbed—*"Until Shiloh come"* (Genesis 49:10). The law-giver of Israel, who was "king in Jeshurun," spoke of Him, for Moses said, "A prophet shall the Lord your God raise up unto you, of your brethren, like unto me: Him shall ye hear." (See Deuteronomy 18:15.) David celebrated Him in many a prophetic song—the Anointed of God, the King of Israel; Him to whom all kings shall bow, and all nations call Him blessed. How frequently does he in his Psalms sing about "my Lord"! *"The LORD said to my Lord, Sit You at My right hand, until I make Your enemies Your footstool"* (Psalm 110:1). But need we stop to tell you of Isaiah, who spoke of His passion, and *"saw His glory"* (John 12:41)? of Jeremiah, of Ezekiel, of Daniel, of Micah, of Malachi, and of all the rest of the prophets, who stood with their eyes strained, looking through the dim mists of futurity, until the weeks of prophecy should be fulfilled—until the sacred day should arrive, when Jesus Christ should come in the flesh? They were all waiting for the consolation of Israel. And, now, good old Simeon, standing on the verge of the period when Christ would come, with expectant eyes looked out for Him…. We are, we trust, some of us, in the same posture as Simeon. We have climbed the staircase of the Christian virtues, from whence we look for that blessed hope, the coming of our Lord Jesus Christ.

DAY 1

EVENING

"But they that wait upon the Lord
shall renew their strength."
—Isaiah 40:31

Every form of human strength must of necessity spend itself, for the world of which it forms a part decays, and by and by, like a worn-out vesture, the heavens and the earth shall be rolled up and put away. Some signs of age the creatures show already, but the time will come when their strength shall utterly fail. The reason is that all strength apart from God is derived strength, and is consequently measurable. Yes, apart from God it is not strength at all and consequently must come to an end. The river runs on and the brook fails not, because they come from fountains that are not affected by drought, but cisterns are dried and reservoirs fail because they have no springing well at the bottom of them, and if the pipes which supply them cease to flow, they are soon left dry as a threshing-floor. Pools which are not self-supplied are always liable to be exhausted as the water is drained from them.… Our own righteousness, our own thoughts, our own religiousness, our own prayers, resolves, attainments, achievements—everything that is of ourselves, must sooner or later prove themselves to be but human, and over all things human it is best to write, *"Vanity of vanities; all is vanity"* (Ecclesiastes 1:2). Mingled with all things human there are portions of that all-dissolving acid which fell upon man's nature when infinite justice said, *"Dust you are, and to dust shall you return"* (Genesis 3:19). On the other hand, what a contrast there is as to divine strength! That never fails. It seems almost a superfluity to say as much as that; it abides in joyous fullness, never in the least diminished. With God there are no years to make Him decline with age, no labors to tax His powers. With God our lives are but as the swing of the pendulum. A thousand years in His sight are passed away as a watch in the night. Millions of ages are nothing to Him. He was God when as yet this sun, and moon, and all these stars slept in His thoughts like unborn forests in an acorn cup. And He will be God when all this brief creation shall melt back to nothing as a moment's foam dissolves into the wave that bore it and is lost forever.

DAY 2

MORNING

"And I will put enmity between you and the woman,
and between your seed and her seed."
—Genesis 3:15

These words were not directly spoken to Adam and Eve, but they were directed distinctly to the Serpent himself, and that by way of punishment to him for what he had done. It was a day of cruel triumph to him. Such joy as his dark mind is capable of had filled him, for he had indulged his malice, and gratified his spite. He had in the worst sense destroyed a part of God's works, he had introduced sin into the new world, he had stamped the human race with his own image, and gained new forces to promote rebellion and to multiply transgression, and therefore he felt that sort of gladness which a fiend can know who bears a hell within him. But now God comes in, takes up the quarrel personally, and causes him to be disgraced on the very battlefield upon which he had gained a temporary success. God tells the Dragon that He will undertake to deal with him; this quarrel shall not be between the serpent and man, but between God and the Serpent. God says, in solemn words, *"I will put enmity between you and* the woman, and between your seed and her seed," and He promised that there shall rise in fullness of time a champion, who, though He suffer, shall smite in a vital part the power of evil, and bruise the Serpent's head.... Perhaps, however, by thus obliquely giving the promise, the Lord meant to say, "Not for your sakes do I this, O fallen man and woman, nor for the sake of your descendants; but for My own name and honor's sake, that it be not profaned and blasphemed among the fallen spirits. I undertake to repair the mischief which has been caused by the Tempter, that My name and My glory may not be diminished among the immortal spirits who look down upon the scene." All this would be very humbling but yet consolatory to our parents if they thought of it, seeing that mercy given for God's sake is always to our troubled apprehension more sure than any favor which could be promised to us for our own sake. The divine sovereignty and glory afford us a stronger foundation of hope than merit.

EVENING

"It shall bruise your head,
and you shall bruise His heel."
—Genesis 3:15

This was all that Adam had by way of revelation, and all that Abel had received. This one lone star shone in Abel's sky; he looked up to it and he believed. By its light he spelled out "sacrifice," and therefore he brought of the firstlings of his flock and laid them on the altar, and proved in his own person how the seed of the Serpent hated the seed of the woman, for his brother slew him for his testimony. Although Enoch the seventh from Adam prophesied concerning the second advent, yet he does not appear to have uttered anything new concerning the first coming, so that still this one promise remained as man's sole word of hope. The torch which flamed within the gates of Eden just before man was driven forth lit up the world to all believers until the Lord was pleased to give more light, and to renew and enlarge the revelation of His covenant, when He spoke to His servant Noah. Those hoary fathers who lived before the flood rejoiced in the mysterious language of our text, and resting on it, they died in faith. Nor, brethren, must you think it a slender revelation, for, if you attentively consider, it is wonderfully full of meaning.... Observe that here is the grand mystery of incarnation.... Here, too, the great fact of the sufferings of Christ is clearly foretold—*"you shall bruise His heel."* Within the compass of those words we find the whole story of our Lord's sorrows from Bethlehem to Calvary. *"It shall bruise your head"*: there is the breaking of Satan's regal power, there is the clearing away of sin, there is the destruction of death by resurrection, there is the leading of captivity captive in the ascension, there is the victory of truth in the world through the descent of the Spirit, and there is the latter-day glory in which Satan shall be bound, and there is, lastly, the casting of the Evil One and all his followers into the lake of fire. The conflict and the conquest are both in the compass of these few fruitful words. They may not have been fully understood by those who first heard them, but to us they are now full of light.

DAY 3

MORNING

*"Wait on the LORD: be of good courage,
and He shall strengthen your heart."*
—Psalm 27:14

A true servant is anxious to know what his master wishes him to do and, when he once knows it, he is happy to undertake it and carry it through. In great houses, certain servants inquire of the master in the morning, "Sir, what are your orders for the day?" Imitate this and when you rise in the morning, always wait upon your Lord to know what are His commands for the day. Say, "Show me what You would have me do. Teach me Your way, O Lord. Lead me in a plain path. Inform me as to what to seek and what to shun, for my will is to do Your will in all things." Notice how maidservants watch their mistresses when they are waiting at table or serving about the house. A word is enough and sometimes a look or a nod of the head is all the direction needed. So should it be with us— we should eagerly desire to know the mind of the Lord and carefully watch for indications of it. As the eyes of a maiden are unto the hand of her mistress, so should our eyes wait upon the Lord our God. (See Psalm 123:2.) We, who are the ministers of the Lord Jesus, ought to be looking all around to see what we can do in God's house. Good servants do not need to be told of every little thing—they have their master's interest at heart and they perceive what should be done and they do it. Oh, to be always waiting to do yet more and more for Jesus! I would go up and down my Master's house, seeing what I can do for His little children whom I delight to cherish. What part of the house needs sweeping and cleaning, that I may quietly go about it! What part of the table needs to be furnished with food, that I may bring out as His steward things new and old. What there is to be done for my Master toward those who are without and what is to be done for those already in His family. You will never be short of work if with your whole heart you wait upon the Lord.

_____

_____

_____

_____

_____

_____

DAY 3

EVENING

"Wait, I say, on the Lord."
—Psalm 27:14

Our heart is strengthened by waiting upon God because we thus receive a mysterious strength through the incoming of the eternal Spirit into our souls. No man can explain this, but many of us know what it is. We do not know how the Holy Spirit operates, but we are conscious that after a season of prayer we are often much refreshed and feel as if we had been made young again. We have gone in before the Lord haggard and worn, desponding and (shame upon us, we must add) ready to give up, turn tail, and run away. We have not long drawn near God before we have felt our spirit revive. Though our approach was mostly a groan, yet we did wait upon the Lord, and the eternal strength came into us. How wonderfully do the secret springs of omnipotence break into the feeble soul and fill it with might in the inner man. Through the sacred anointing of the Holy Spirit we have been made to shout for joy. We have been so glad in the Lord that we could not contain our joy. He that made us has put His hand a second time to the work and restored to us the joy of His salvation, filled our emptiness, removed our weakness, and triumphed in us gloriously. The poor harp which had been long played upon could not at length yield music to its owner's hand. In vain the bardic fingers roamed over the strings; the more heavily they were struck, the more discordant were the sounds. The harp was taken from the hall and laid aside in a quiet chamber and there its Maker came to deal with it. He knew its frame and understood the art of tuning it. He put new strings here and there and set the rest aright, and the next time the harper laid his fingers among the strings, pure music floated forth and flooded the palace with melody. Where discord had peopled the air with evil spirits, all was changed and it seemed as though angels leaped forth with silver wings from every chord. Yes, go to your God, poor soul, when you are out of order. Wait on the Lord and He will strengthen your heart by His mysterious power.

DAY 4

MORNING

"Awake, awake, Deborah: awake, awake, utter a song: arise, Barak, and lead your captivity captive."
—Judges 5:12

What is there that we need to awaken if we would praise God? I reply, we ought to arouse all the bodily powers. Our flesh is sluggish; we have been busy with the world, our limbs have grown fatigued, but there is power in divine joy to arouse even the body itself, to make the heavy eyelids light, to reanimate the drowsy eye, and quicken the weary brain. We should call upon our bodies to awake, especially our tongue, "the glory of our frame." Let it put itself in tune like David's harp of old. Surely we should call on all our mental powers to awake. Wake up, my memory, and find matter for the song. Tell what God has done for me in days gone by. Awake, my judgment, and give measure to the music. Come forth, my understanding, and weigh His loving-kindness in scales, and His goodness in the balances. See if you can count the small dust of His mercies. See if you can understand the riches unsearchable which He has given to you in that unspeakable gift of Christ Jesus my Lord. Awake, my imagination, and dance to the holy melody. Gather pictures from all worlds. Bid sun and moon stay in their courses, and join in your new song. But especially let us cry to all the graces of our spirit—*"Awake."* Wake up, my love, for you must strike the keynote and lead the strain. Wake up, my hope, and join hands with your sister, love, and sing of blessings yet to come. Sing of my dying hour, when He shall be with me on my couch. Sing of the rising morning, when my body shall leap from its tomb into her Savior's arms! Sing of the expected advent, for which you look with delight! And oh, my soul, sing of that heaven which He has gone before to prepare for you. And you, my faith, awake also. Sing of the promise sure and certain. Then let us wake up the energy of all those powers—the energy of the body, the energy of the mind, the energy of the spirit. You know what it is to do thing coldly, weakly. As well might we not praise at all! You know also what it is to praise God passionately—to throw energy into all the song, and so to exult in His name. So do you, each one of you, this day.

_____

_____

_____

_____

_____

_____

DAY 4

EVENING

"My soul, wait you only upon God;
for my expectation is from Him."
—Psalm 62:5

Perhaps the most miserable people in the world are the very careful ones. You that are so anxious about what shall happen tomorrow that you cannot enjoy the pleasures of today, you who have such a peculiar cast of mind that you suspect every star to be a comet, and imagine that there must be a volcano in every grassy mead, you that are more attracted by the spots in the sun than by the sun himself, and more amazed by one sear leaf upon the tree than by all the verdure of the woods—you that make more of your troubles than you could do of your joys, I say, I think you belong to the most miserable of men. David says to his soul, "My soul, be careful for nothing except God; cast all your care on him; He cares for you, and make this your great concern, to love and serve Him; and then you need care for nothing else at all." Oh! there are many of you people that go picking your way all through this world afraid to put one foot down before another, because you fear you will be in danger. If you had grace just to turn your eye to God, you might walk straight on in confidence, and say, "Though I should tread on hell itself at the next step, yet if God bade me tread there it would be heaven to me." There is nothing like the faith that can leave care with God and have no thought but how to please Him…. Oh, happy is the man who says, "I am a gentleman commoner upon the bounties of providence. Let God send me little, it will be enough; let Him send me much, it will not be too much, for I will divide my wealth with those who have less. I will trust to Him. He has said, 'Your bread shall be given you, and your water shall be sure.' (See Isaiah 34:16.) Then let famine come, I shall not starve; let the brook dry up, He will open the bottles of heaven and give me drink. Whatever shall happen to this world, yet shall I be secure against all ills."

_____

_____

_____

_____

_____

DAY 5

MORNING

"Behold, a virgin shall conceive, and bear a Son, and shall call His name Immanuel."
—Isaiah 7:14

In the worst times we are to preach Christ and to look to Christ! In Jesus there is a remedy for the direst of diseases and a rescue from the darkest of despairs. Ahaz…was in great danger, for he was attacked by two kings, each one stronger than himself. But the Lord promised him deliverance and commanded him to choose a sign either in the heights, or in the depths. This, under a hypocritical presence, he refused to do and therefore the Lord chose as His own token the appearance of the heavenly Deliverer who would be God and yet born of a woman. *"Behold, a virgin shall conceive, and bear a Son, and shall call His name Immanuel."* He was to eat butter and honey, like other children in that land of milk and honey, and yet He was to be the Mighty God, the everlasting Father, and the Prince of Peace. We see here Godhead in union with manhood! We behold Jesus, man "of the substance of His mother," and yet, "God over all, blessed forever." Surely this God-appointed sign was both in the depth and in the height above; the Man of Sorrows, the Son of the Highest. This vision was the light of the age of Ahaz. It is God's comfort to troubled hearts in all ages; it is God's sign of grace to us this morning. The sure hope of sinners and the great joy of saints is the incarnate Lord, Immanuel, God with us! May He be your joy and mine even this day; He it is who is the great light of the people who dwell in the land of the shadow of death! If any among you are in that dreary land, may He be light and life to you!... In Judah's trouble, the Virgin-Born was God's token that He would deliver and speedily; for in less time than it would take such a child to reach years of knowledge, both Judah's royal adversaries would be gone. The sign was good for Ahaz, but it is better far for us. Behold the incarnate Son of God born of Mary at Bethlehem; what can this intend for us but divine grace?

_____

_____

_____

_____

_____

_____

EVENING

"This is the confidence that we have in Him, that,
if we ask any thing according to His will, He hears us."
—1 John 5:14

Be humbled and pray God to make you like the importunate widow, for so only will you prevail. But at the same time let me remind you that if your prayers be sincere it shall often happen that even their weakness shall not destroy them. He may rebuke the unbelief of your prayer, and yet in infinite mercy He may exceed His promise. Further, I have no doubt many of God's people cannot think their prayers will be heard, because they have had as yet such very few manifest replies. You say you have had no answers! How know you? God may have answered you, though you have not seen the answer. God has not promised to give you the particular mercy in kind, but He will give it you somehow or other.... Then there are so many, again, who pray in a legal spirit. Why do you pray? Because it is your duty? A child does not cry because the time to cry has come, nor does a sick man groan because it is the hour of groaning, but they cry and groan because they cannot help it. When the newborn nature says, "Let us draw nigh unto God," then is the time and the place. A legal spirit would prevent our expecting answers to prayer. Inconsistencies after prayer, and a failure to press our suit, will bring us to doubt the power of prayer. If we do not plead with God again and again, we shall not keep up our faith that God hears us. Let us believe in God's answering prayer, I mean those of us who have believed in Jesus; and that because we have God's promise for us. Hear what He says, *"You shall make your prayer to Him, and He shall hear you"* (Job 22:27). Again, prayer must be answered, because of the character of God our Father. Will He let His children cry and not hear them? He hears the young ravens, and will He not hear His own people? Then think of the efficacy of the blood of Jesus. When you pray it is the blood that speaks. Think, again, that Jesus pleads. Shall the Father deny the Son? Besides, the Holy Spirit Himself is the Author of your prayers. Will God indite the desire, and then not hear it?

DAY 6

MORNING

*"Through the tender mercy of our God; whereby the
dayspring from on high has visited us."*
—Luke 1:78

God made heaven and earth with His fingers, but He
gave His Son with His heart in order that He might save
sinners…. He has not merely pitied us from a distance,
and sent us relief by way of the ladder which Jacob saw,
but He has Himself visited us. God does not come to us
in Christ, or by His Spirit, as a tempest, as when He came
from Paran, with ten thousand of His holy ones, in all the
pomp of His fiery law; but He has visited us as smiling
morn, which in gentle glory floods the world with joy.
He has come, moreover, not as a blaze which will soon
die down, but as a light which will last our day, yes, last
forever. After the long, dark, and cold night of our misery,
the Lord comes in the fittest and most effectual manner;
neither as lightning, nor candle, nor flaming meteor, but
as the sun which begins the day. The visitation of the Lord
to us is as the dayspring, because it suits our eye. Day,
when it first breaks in the east, has not the blaze of burning noon about it; but peeps forth as a grey light, which

gradually increases. So did Christ come; dimly, as it were, at first, at Bethlehem, but by and by He will appear in all the glory of the Father. So does the Spirit of God come to us in gradual progress. The revelation of God to each individual is made in form and manner tenderly agreeable to the condition and capacity of the favored one. He shows us just so much of Himself as to delight us without utterly overwhelming us with the excess of brightness. The visits of God are like the dayspring, because they end our darkness. Our night is ended once for all when we behold God visiting us in Christ Jesus. Our day may cloud over, but night will not return. Christ's coming into the world is as the morning light, because He comes with such a largeness of present blessing. He is the Light which lightens every man. The dayspring is not the noon, but it is the sure guarantee of it; and so the first advent is the pledge of the glory to be revealed.

EVENING

*"The scepter shall not depart from Judah, nor a
lawgiver from between his feet, until Shiloh come."*
—Genesis 49:10

Jacob's name for Jesus was "Shiloh"; and it is so long ago
since he called Him Shiloh that I do not wonder that we
have almost forgotten the meaning of it…. Some main-
tain that the word "Shiloh" signifies "sent." Like that
word you have in the New Testament, "[He] *said to them,
go wash in the pool of Siloam, (which is, by interpretation,
Sent)"* (John 9:7), you observe the likeness between the
words *Siloam* and *Shiloh*. They think that the words have
the same meaning; in which case *Shiloh* here would mean
the same as *Messiah*, the sent one—and would indicate
that Jesus Christ was the messenger, the sent one of God,
and came to us, not at His own instance, and at His own
will, but commissioned by the Most High, authorized and
anointed to that end. Here let us stop a minute. We rejoice
to know that, whatever this title means, it is quite certain
Jesus was sent. It is a very precious thing to know that we
have a Savior; but often and often it has cheered my heart
to think that this dear Savior who came to save me did

not come as an amateur, unauthorized from the courts of heaven, but He came with the credentials of the eternal Father, so that, whatever He has done, we may be sure He has done it in the name of God. Jehovah will never repudiate that which Jesus has accomplished…. The interpretation, however, which has the most support, and which I think has the fairest claim to be accorded correct, is that which derives the word "Shiloh" from the same root as the word "Salem." This makes it signify peace. "Until the peace, or the peace-bearer, or the peace-giver," or, if you like it better, "the rest, or the rest-maker—shall come." … Do you know what rest means? Such "peace, peace," such perfect peace as he has whose soul is stayed; because he trusts, as the prophet Isaiah has it. Here is rest! Man may well take his rest when he has nothing to do, when it is all done for him. And that is the gospel. The world's way of salvation is "Do," God's way of salvation is, "It is all done for you; accept and believe."

_____

_____

_____

_____

_____

_____

MORNING

"He was rich."
—2 Corinthians 8:9

Think not that our Savior began to live when He was born of the Virgin Mary; imagine not that He dates His existence from the manger at Bethlehem; remember He is the eternal, He is before all things, and by Him all things consist. There was never a time in which there was not God. And just so, there was never a period in which there was not Christ Jesus our Lord. He is self-existent, has no beginning of days, neither end of years; He is the immortal, invisible, the only wise God, our Savior. Now, in the past eternity which had elapsed before His mission to this world, we are told that Jesus Christ was rich; and to those of us who believe His glories and trust in His divinity, it is not hard to see how He was so. Jesus was rich in possessions. Lift up your eye, believer, and for a moment review the riches of my Lord Jesus, before He condescended to become poor for you. Behold Him, sitting upon His throne and declaring His own all-sufficiency. "If I were hungry, I would not tell thee, for the cattle on a thousand hills are mine. Mine are the hidden treasures of gold; mine are the pearls that the diver can not reach; mine every precious thing that earth has seen." The Lord Jesus might have said, "I can stretch my scepter from the east even to the west, and all is mine; the whole of this world, and yon worlds that glitter in far off space, all are mine…." Jesus, who is he that could look upon the brow of Your Majesty, who is he that could comprehend the strength of the arm of Your might? You are God, You are infinite, and we poor, finite things, are lost in You. The insect of an hour cannot comprehend Your self. We bow before You, we adore You; You are God over all, blessed forever. But as for the comprehension of Your boundless riches, as for being able to tell Your treasures, or to reckon up Your wealth, that were impossible. All we know is, that the wealth of God, that the treasures of the infinite, that the riches of eternity, were all Your own: You were rich beyond all thought.

EVENING

"Yet for your sakes He became poor."
—2 Corinthians 8:9

Do you see Him as on that day of heaven's eclipse He did ungird His majesty?... Where sleeps the newborn King? Had He the best room in Caesar's palace? Has a cradle of gold been prepared for him, and pillows of down, on which to rest His head? No, where the ox fed, in the dilapidated stable, in the manger, there the Savior lies, swathed in the swaddling bands of the children of poverty! Nor there does He rest long; on a sudden His mother must carry Him to Egypt; He goes there, and becomes a stranger in a strange land. When He comes back, see Him that made the worlds handle the hammer and the nails, assisting His father in the trade of a carpenter!... As for His food, He oftentimes did hunger; and always was dependent upon the charity of others for the relief of His wants! He who scattered the harvest over the broad acres of the world, had not sometimes wherewithal to stay the pangs of hunger? He who dug the springs of the ocean, sat upon a well and said to a Samaritan woman, "Give me to drink!" He rode in no chariot, He walked His weary way, foot sore, over the flints of Galilee! He had not where to lay His head. He looked upon the fox as it hurried to its burrow, and the fowl as it went to its resting-place, and He said, *"Foxes have holes, and the birds of the air have nests; but the Son of man has not where to lay His head"* (Luke 9:58). He who had once been waited on by angels, becomes the servant of servants, takes a towel, girds Himself, and washes His disciples' feet! He who was once honored with the hallelujahs of ages, is now spit upon and despised! He who was loved by His Father, and had abundance of the wealth of affection, could say, *"He that eats bread with Me has lifted up his heel against Me"* (John 3:18). Oh, for words to picture the humiliation of Christ! What leagues of distance between Him that sat upon the throne, and Him that died upon the cross! Oh, who can tell the mighty chasm between yonder heights of glory, and the cross of deepest woe! Trace Him, Christian, He has left you His manger to show you how God came down to man.

DAY 8
MORNING

"As for me, I will behold Your face in righteousness:
I shall be satisfied, when I awake, with Your likeness."
—Psalm 17:15

Have I not seen my Father's face here below? Yes, I have, *"through a glass, darkly"* (1 Corinthians 13:12). But has not the Christian sometimes beheld Him, when in His heavenly moments earth is gone, and the mind is stripped of matter? There are some seasons when the gross materialism dies away, and when the ethereal fire within blazes up so high that it almost touches the fire of heaven. There are seasons, when in some retired spot, calm and free from all earthly thought, we have put our shoes from off our feet because the place whereon we stood was holy ground; and we have talked with God! Even as Enoch talked with Him so has the Christian held intimate communion with His Father. He has heard His love whispers, he has told out his heart, poured out his sorrows and his groans before Him. But after all he has felt that he has not beheld His face in righteousness. There was so much sin to darken the eyes, so much folly, so much frailty, that we could not get a clear prospect of our Jesus. But here the psalmist says, *"I will behold Your face in righteousness."* When that illustrious day shall arise, and I shall see my Savior face to face, I shall see Him *"in righteousness."* The Christian in heaven will not have so much as a speck upon his garment; he will be pure and white; yes, on the earth he is "Pure through Jesus' blood, and white as angels are." But in heaven that whiteness shall be more apparent. Now, it is sometimes smoked by earth, and covered with the dust of this poor carnal world; but in heaven he will have brushed himself, and washed his wings and made them clean; and then will he see God's face in righteousness. My God; I believe I shall stand before Your face as pure as You are Yourself, for I shall have the righteousness of Jesus Christ there shall be upon me the righteousness of a God. *"I will behold Your face in righteousness."* O Christian, can you enjoy this?

DAY 8

EVENING

*"As a beast goes down into the valley, the Spirit of the
Lord caused him to rest: so did You lead Your people,
to make yourself a glorious name."*
—Isaiah 63:14

God is glorious in the history of Israel. God is glorious
in the history of His church. God is glorious in the history
of every believer. The life of a true believer is a glorious
life. For himself he claims no honor, but by his holy life
he brings great glory to God. There is more glory to God
in every poor man and woman saved by grace, and in the
one unknown obscure person, washed in the Redeemer's
blood, than in all the songs of cherubim and seraphim,
who know nothing of free grace and dying love. So you
see, beloved, the motive of God in all that He did; and
I dwell upon it, though briefly, yet with much emphasis,
because this is a motive that can never alter. What if the
church of today be reduced to a very low condition, and
the truth seems to be ebbing out from her shores, while
a long stretch of the dreary mud of modern invention
lies reeking in the nostrils of God; yet He that wrought
such wonders, to make Himself a name, still has the same

object in view. He will be glorious. He will have men know that He is God, and beside Him there is none else.... O brethren, He is a jealous God still; and when the precious blood of Christ is insulted, God hears it, and forgets it not. When the inspiration of the blessed Book is denied, the Holy Spirit hears it and is grieved, and He will yet bestir Himself to defend His truth. When we hear the truth that we love, the dearest and most sacred revelations from our God, treated with a triviality that is nothing less than profane, if we are indignant, so is He, and shall not God avenge His own elect which cry day and night to Him? I tell you that He will avenge them speedily, though He bear long with His adversaries. God's motive is His own glory.... Here, then, is the hope of the people of God, the constant, persistent, invariable motive of God to make Himself glorious in the eyes of men.

DAY 9

MORNING

"Men shall be blessed in Him:
all nations shall call Him blessed."
—Psalm 72:17

There is one name that will last when all others shall have died out; and that name is connected with blessing, and only with blessing. Jesus Christ came into the world on purpose to bless men. Men, as a race, find in Him a blessing wide as the world. While He was here He blessed, and cursed not. All around Him, both by speech, and act, and glance, and thought, He was an incarnate blessing. All that came to Him, unless they willfully rejected Him, obtained blessings at His hands. The home of His infancy, the friends of His youth, the comrades of His manhood, He blessed unsparingly. To bless men, He labored. To bless men, He parted with everything, and became poor. To bless men, at last He died. Those outstretched hands upon the cross are spread wide in benediction, and they are fastened there as if they would remain outstretched till the whole world is blessed. Our Lord's resurrection from the dead brings blessings to mankind. Redemption from the grave, and life eternal, He has won for us. He waited on earth a while, until He ascended, blessing men as He went up. His last attitude below the skies was that of pronouncing a blessing upon His disciples. He is gone into the glory; but He has not ceased to bless our race. The Holy Spirit came among us soon after the ascension, because Jesus had received gifts for men; yes, for the rebellious also. The wonderful blessings which are comprised in the work, person, and offices of the Holy Spirit—all these come to us through Jesus Christ, the ever-blessed and ever-blessing One. Still He loves to bless. Standing at the helm of all affairs, He guides the tiller of Providence with a view to the blessing of His chosen. He spends His time still in making intercession for transgressors, that the blessing of God may rest upon them; while His Spirit, who is His Vicegerent here below, is evermore occupied with blessing the sons of men. Our Lord Jesus will soon come a second time, and in that glorious hour, though His left hand must deal out justice, still His right hand will lavish blessing…. From the beginning, throughout all eternity, the Lord Jesus blesses men.

DAY 9

EVENING

"And they shall call His name Immanuel,
which being interpreted is, God with us."
—Matthew 1:23

God has, in very deed, come near to us in very close association. He must have done so, for He has taken upon Himself our nature, literally our nature: flesh, blood, bone, everything that made a body; mind, heart, soul, memory, imagination, judgement, everything that makes a rational man.... Being with us in our nature, God was with us in all our life's pilgrimage. Scarcely can you find a halting place in the march of life at which Jesus has not paused, or a weary league which He has not traversed. From the gate of entrance even to the door which closes life's way, the footprints of Jesus may be traced. Were you in the cradle? He was there. Were you a child under parental authority? Christ was also a boy in the home at Nazareth. Have you entered upon life's battle? Your Lord and Master did the same, and though He lived not to old age, yet through incessant toil and suffering, He bore the marred visage which attends a battered old age. Are you alone? So was He, in the wilderness and on the mountain's side, and in the garden's gloom. Do you mix in public society? So did He labor in the thickest crowds. Where can you find yourself, on the hilltop, or in the valley, on the land or on the sea, in the daylight or in darkness—where, I say, can you be without discovering that Jesus has been there before you? What the world has said of her great poet we might with far more truth say of our Redeemer— "A man so various that he seemed to be / Not one, but all mankind's epitome." One harmonious man He was, and yet all saintly lives seem to be condensed in His. Two believers may be very unlike each other, and yet both will find that Christ's life has in it points of likeness to their own. One shall be rich and another shall be poor. One actively laborious and another patiently suffering, and yet each man, in studying the history of the Savior, shall be able to say—His pathway ran hard by my own. He was made in all points like to His brethren. (See Hebrews 2:17.) How charming is the fact that our Lord is "God with us," not here and there, and now and then, but forever.

DAY 10

MORNING

"Out of Egypt have I called My Son."
—Matthew 2:15

Friendly Egypt, sheltering Egypt, was not Israel's inheritance. God gave them no portion even in the land of Goshen by a covenant of salt. They might tarry there for a while, but out of it they must come, as it is written, *"You have brought a vine out of Egypt"* (Psalm 80:8). The best side of the world when it seems warmest and most tender to us is not the place where we may lie down with comfort. The bosom of our God—that is the true shelter of His people, and there we must find rest. If we are dwelling in the world, and are tempted to be of the world, and to take up with the riches of Egypt, we must by grace be taught to cast all this behind our back, for we have not our portion in this life, neither can we have our inheritance until we enter upon the life that is to come. Jacob said on his deathbed, "Bury me not, I pray you, in Egypt." And Joseph gave commandment concerning his bones that they should not remain in Pharaoh's land. Even so the saints of God are weary of the world's dominions; they tremble like a bird out of Egypt. Not in Egypt would God reveal Himself to His people.

What says He? "Come you out from among them: be you separate and I will be a Father to you, and you shall be My sons and daughters." (See 1 Corinthians 6:17.) When He called Israel His son, it is in connection with this coming out. *"Out of Egypt have I called My Son."* And you and I must be fetched out from the world and all its associations, and truly severed from it, if we are ever to come to know the Lord our God. In Egypt God was not known, but *"in Judah is God known: His name is great in Israel"* (Psalm 76:1). His people must not permanently reside in a strange country. The land of tombs was no fit home for a living people whose God was the living God. Therefore it is written, *"Out of Egypt have I called My Son"* and the heathen knew it, for they said one to another, *"Behold, there is a people come out of Egypt"* (Numbers 22:11).

EVENING

"When Israel was a child, then I loved him,
and called My son out of Egypt."
—Hosea 11:1

God calls Israel His son. What for? Because within that nation lay that seed, which afterwards was known as the Well-Beloved, the Son of the Highest. They were the shell and therefore to be preserved for the sake of the Blessed One who, according to the flesh, lay within the race. I do not think the Lord would have cared about the Jews more than any other nation, if it had not been that in due time He was to be born of them, even He in whom is His delight, that choice one of the Father, the Son whom He loves. So when He brought His son out of Egypt, it means first, that He rescued the external, nominal, outward sonship. But the core, the living core within, is this Son, this true Son of whom the Lord said, putting all others aside, *"This is My beloved Son, in whom I am well pleased"* (Matthew 3:17). And the passage, if I had time to show you, could not be limited to Israel, for if it had been, it would lose much of its accuracy. Why, do you think, the passage was made so obscure? For it is confessedly obscure, and anyone reading it without the spiritual teaching which Matthew received would never have perceived that Christ was going down into Egypt to fulfill that word. I take it, the reason of the obscurity was this—that its fulfillment might be of the Lord alone.... Remember one thing; that all the words of God in the Old Testament and the New refer to Christ, and what is more, all the works of God have an opened window towards Christ. Yes, I say that in the creation of the world the central thought of God was His Son Jesus, and He made the world with a view to His death, resurrection, and glorious reign. From every gnat that dances in the summer sunbeam up to the great leviathan in the sea, the whole design of the world works toward the Seed in which the earth is blessed. In providence it is just the same, every event, from the fall of a leaf to the rise of a monarch, is linked with the kingdom of Jesus.

MORNING

*"If there be any consolation in Christ, if any comfort
of love, if any fellowship of the Spirit…."*
—Philippians 2:1

If ever your minds dwell with sadness upon the fact that we are at this day absent from the Lord, because we are present in the body, think of the great truth that Jesus Christ of old had delights with the sons of men, and He delights to commune and have fellowship with His people now. Remember that your Lord and Master appeared to Abraham in the plains of Mamre under the disguise of a pilgrim. Abraham was a pilgrim and Christ, to show His sympathy with His servant, became a pilgrim, too! Did He not also appear to Jacob at the brook Jabbok? Jacob was a wrestler, and Jesus appears there as a wrestler, too. Did He not stand before Moses under the guise and figure of a flame in the midst of a bush? Was not Moses at the very time, the representative of a people who were like a bush burning with fire and yet not consumed? Did He not stand before Joshua—Joshua the leader of Israel's troops, and did He not appear to him as the captain of the Lord's host? And do you not well remember that when the three holy children walked in the midst of the fiery furnace, He was in the midst of the fire, too—not as a king—but as one in the fire with them? Cheer, then, your heart with this consoling inference! If Christ appeared to His servants in the olden time, and manifested Himself to them as bone of their bone and flesh of their flesh—in all their trials and their troubles—He will do no less for you today! He will be with you in passing through the fire—He will be your rock, your shield, and your high tower. He will be your song, your banner, and your crown of rejoicing. Fear not, He who visited His saints of old will surely not be long absent from His children today—His delights are still with His people, and still will He walk with us through this weary wilderness! Surely this makes Christ a most blessed consolation for His Israel!

DAY 11

EVENING

"To them that look for Him shall He appear the second time without sin to salvation."
—Hebrews 9:28

As we are here twice—once in a life of probation, and a second time in the day of judgment; so Christ shall be here twice—once in His life of suffering, and then again in His hour of triumph, and the two comings of Christ have some degree of likeness. The advents shall be like each other in the fact that they shall both be according to promise. The promise of the first coming of Christ was that which made glad the early believers. *"Your father Abraham rejoiced to see My day: and he saw it, and was glad"* (John 8:56). The epitaph inscribed upon the slab which covers the sepulcher of the early saints has written upon it, *"These all died in faith, not having received the promises, but having seen them afar off"* (Hebrews 11:13). And today, we believe that Christ is to come according to promise. We think we have abundant evidence in the words that were uttered by the lips of inspired prophets and seers, and more especially, from the enraptured pen of John in Patmos. Do they not testify that Christ shall surely come?

We now, like Abraham of old, do see His day; our eyes catch the coming splendor; our soul is overwhelmed with the approaching glory! Did the Jew look for Messiah, the Prince? So do we! Did he expect Him to reign? So do we! In fact, the very Prince, for whom Israel now looks in all her hardness of heart, is He whom we expect! They doubt Messiah's first advent, and they look for Him to come as the fairest among ten thousand, the Prince of the kings of the earth. Hail, Israel! In this your Gentile sister is agreed! She looks for Him to come in the same form and fashion. And when His coming shall have removed the scales from the blind eyes of Israel's tribes, then the fullness of the Gentiles shall, with Abraham's seed, praise and magnify the Lamb once slain, who comes the second time as the Lion of the tribe of Judah! In both cases we think the advent of Christ fully promised.

MORNING

"The Word was made flesh, and dwelt among us."
—John 1:14

That God should make a creature out of nothing is certainly a marvelous manifestation of power, but that God should enter into that creature, and should take it into intimate union with His own nature—this is the strangest of all acts of condescending love! Indeed, so marvelous is it, that in all the heathen mythologies…in their theology, we do find instances of the gods appearing in the likeness of men—yet never do we find anything like the hypostatical union of the two natures in the person of Christ. Human wisdom, in its most happy moments, has never risen to anything like the thought of deity espousing manhood that man might be redeemed! To you and to me, the marvel lies in the motive which prompted the incarnation. What could it have been that brought Immanuel to such a stoop as this? What unrivalled, indescribable, unutterable love was this that made Him leave His Father's glory, the adoration of angels, and all the hallowed joy of heaven, that He might be made a man like ourselves, to suffer, to bleed, to die? … That He should be the associate of the worst of men, that He should be called the friend of publicans and sinners, so perfectly incarnating Himself and condescending so low that He comes to the very lowest state of humanity—all this, my brothers and sisters, is condescension concerning which words fail me! A prince who puts aside his crown, and clothes himself with beggar's rags to investigate the miseries of his country, is but a worm condescending to his fellow worm. An angel that should lay aside his beauty, and become decrepit and lame, and walk the streets in pain and poverty to bless the race of man were nothing, for this were but a creature humbling himself to creatures a little lower than himself; but, here is the Creator taking the creature into union with Himself! The Immortal becoming mortal, the Infinite an infant, the Omnipotent taking weakness, even human weakness, into union with His own person! We may truly say of Jesus that He was weak as the dust, and yet, as mighty as the eternal God. He was subject to suffering, and yet, God over all blessed forever. O the depth of the love of Jesus!

DAY 12

EVENING

"And we beheld His glory,
the glory as of the only begotten of the Father."
—John 1:14

See the glory of manhood now restored! Man was but a little lower than the angels, and had dominion over the fowl of the air, and over the fish of the sea. That royalty he lost; the crown was taken from his head by the hand of sin, and the beauty of the image of God was dashed by his rebellion. But all this is given back to us! We see Jesus, who was made a little lower than the angels, for the suffering of death, crowned with glory and honor; and, at this day, all things are put under Him, waiting, as He does, and expecting the time, when all His enemies shall be beneath His feet, and the last enemy, Death, shall be destroyed by man—by the very man whom he boasted that he had destroyed! It is our nature, brothers and sisters, Jesus in our manhood, who is now Lord of Providence; it is our nature which has hanging at its belt the keys of heaven, and earth, and hell; it is our nature which sits upon the throne of God at this very day! No angel ever sat upon God's throne, but a man has done it, and is doing it now!

Of no angel was it ever said, "You shall be King of kings, and Lord of lords, they who dwell in the wilderness shall bow before you, and your enemies shall lick the dust." (See Psalm 72.) But this is said of a man! It is the man who shall judge the world in righteousness; a man who shall distribute crowns of reward—a man who shall denounce, "Depart, you cursed" (see Matthew 25:41); a man, the thunder of whose words shall make hell shrink with fright! Oh, how glorious is renovated manhood! What an honor it is, my brothers and sisters, to be man, not of the fallen first Adam, but man made in the image of the second Adam! Let us, with all our weaknesses, and infirmities, and imperfections, yet bless and praise God, who made us what we are by His divine grace, for man, in the person of Christ, is second only to God—no, is in such union with God, that he cannot be nearer to Him!

DAY 13

MORNING

"That signs and wonders may be done by the name of Your holy child Jesus."
—Acts 4:30

Why is Christ called a *"holy child"*? We can understand His being called a child while He was so, but why a *"holy child"* now that He is ascended up on high? Why, dear friends, because the character of Christ is more aptly pictured by that of a child than that of a man! If you conceive of a perfectly holy child, you have, then, before you a representation of Christ. There is that in childhood, in holy childhood, which you cannot find even in holy manhood! You note in childhood its simplicity—the absence of all cunning. We dare not in manhood usually wear our heart upon our sleeve as children do; we have lost the trustfulness of our youth, and are upon our guard in society. We have learned by very painful experience to suspect others, and we walk among our fellow men often with our heart locked up with many locks, thinking that, when thieves are abroad, good housekeepers must not leave the door open. We have to practice the wisdom of serpents, as well as the harmlessness of doves. But a child is perfectly guileless; it prattles out its little heart; it has no caution or reserve; it cannot scheme, for it cannot go round about with the skillful words of the politician; it knows not how to spin the web of sophistry; it is plain, transparent, and you see through it. Now, such was Christ! Not foolish, for there is much difference between simplicity and folly. He was never foolish; they who mistook Him for such and sought to entrap Him, soon discovered that the child was a wise child. Still, He is always a child—He tells His heart out everywhere. He eats, He drinks like other men. They call Him a drunk and a wine-bibber; does He, then, from prudential motives, cease to eat and drink as other men? O no! He is quite a child. In everything that He does, there is an artless simplicity. You see through Him, and you can trust Him, because there is trustfulness about His whole nature; He knows what is in man, yet, He does not act with suspicion toward men, but always with simplicity.

DAY 13

EVENING

"The consolation of Israel...."
—Luke 2:25

Oh, how sweet to the soul in distress are the promises of Jesus! For every condition, there is a promise; for every sorrow, there is a cordial; for every wound, there is a balm; for every disease, there is a medicine. If we turn to the Bible, there are promises for all cases. Now, let me appeal to you, my friends. Have you not felt how consoling the promises are to you in seasons of adversity and hours of anguish? Do you not remember some occasion, when your spirits were so broken down that you felt as if you never could have struggled through your woes and sorrows, had not some sweet and precious Word of God come to your help? Minister of the gospel, do you not remember how often you have feared that your message would be of no effect? But you have heard your Master whisper, *"Lo, I am with you always, even to the end of the world"* (Matthew 28:20). Sunday school teacher, have not you said, *"I have labored in vain, I have spent My strength for nothing"* (Isaiah 49:4)? And have you not then heard Jesus say, *"[My Word] shall not return to Me void"* (Isaiah 55:11)? Mourner, you have lost a near relation, have you not heard Jesus then say, *"All things work together for good"* (Romans 8:28)? Softly wipe that tear away, O widow—would not your heart have broken if it had not been for the assurance, *"Your Maker is your husband"* (Isaiah 54:5)? Fatherless child, what would have become of you if you had not turned to the consoling promise, *"Leave your fatherless children…and let your widows trust in Me"* (Jeremiah 49:11)? But why need I tell you, Christian, that there are consoling promises in the Bible? You know there are. I would not sell a leaf of the Bible for a world, nor would I change a promise of it for stars made of gold—"Holy Bible, book divine, / Precious treasure! You are mine." No such comfort can I find as what I derive from you! You are heaven on earth to me, blessed Bible! Verily, if we wait for Christ, we shall find that in His gospel there is consolation for Israel.

DAY 14

MORNING

"But you, Bethlehem Ephratah, though you be little among the thousands of Judah."
—Micah 5:2

The word *Bethlehem* has a double meaning. It signifies "the house of bread," and "the house of war." Ought not Jesus Christ to be born in "the house of bread?" He is the Bread of His people, on which they feed. As our fathers ate manna in the wilderness, so do we live on Jesus here below. Famished by the world, we cannot feed on its shadows. Its husks may gratify the swinish taste of worldlings, for they are swine; but we need something more substantial, and in that blessed Bread of Heaven, made of the bruised body of our Lord Jesus, and baked in the furnace of His agonies, we find a blessed food. No food like Jesus to the desponding soul or to the strongest saint. The very meanest of the family of God goes to Bethlehem for his bread; and the strongest man, who eats strong meat, goes to Bethlehem for it…. But Bethlehem, you house of bread, rightly were you called; for there the Bread of Life was first handed down for man to eat. And it is also called "the house of war," because Christ is to a man "the house of bread," or else "the house of war." While He is food to the righteous, He causes war to the wicked, according to His own word—*"Think not that I am come to send peace on the earth: I am came not to send peace, but a sword. For I am come to set a man at variance against his father, and the daughter against her mother, and the daughter in law against her mother in law. And a man's foes shall be they of his own household"* (Matthew 10:34–36). Sinner! if you do not know Bethlehem as "the house of bread," it shall be to you a "house of war."… Ephratah was the old name of the place which the Jews retained and loved. The meaning of it is, "fruitfulness," or "abundance." Ah! well was Jesus born in the house of fruitfulness; for where comes my fruitfulness and any fruitfulness, my brother, but from Bethlehem? Our poor barren hearts never produced one fruit, or flower, till they were watered with the Savior's blood. It is His incarnation which fattens the soil of our hearts.

DAY 14

EVENING

*"Out of you shall He come forth to Me
that is to be ruler in Israel."*
—Micah 5:2

It is a sweet thought that Jesus Christ did not come forth without His Father's permission, authority, consent, and assistance. He was sent of the Father, that He might be the Savior of men. We are, alas! too apt to forget, that while there are distinctions as to the persons in the Trinity, there are no distinctions of honor; and we do very frequently ascribe the honor of our salvation, or at least the depths of its mercy and the extremity of its benevolence, more to Jesus Christ than we do to the Father. This is a very great mistake. What if Jesus came? Did not His Father send Him? If He was made a child, did not the Holy Spirit beget Him? If He spoke wondrously, did not His Father pour grace into His lips, that He might be an able minister of the new covenant? If His Father did forsake Him when He drank the bitter cup of gall, did He not love Him still? and did He not, by-and-by, after three days, raise Him from the dead, and at last receive Him up on high, leading captivity captive? Ah! beloved, he who knows the Father, and the Son, and the Holy Spirit as he should know them, never sets one before another; he is not more thankful to one than the other; he sees them at Bethlehem, at Gethsemane, and on Calvary, all equally engaged in the work of salvation. "He shall come forth to Me." O Christian, have you put your confidence in the man Christ Jesus? Have you placed your reliance solely on Him? And are you united with Him? Then believe that you are united to the God of heaven; since to the man Christ Jesus you are brother and hold closest fellowship, you are linked thereby with God the eternal, and "the Ancient of days" is your Father and your friend.... Let every thought that you have of Jesus be also connected with the eternal, ever-blessed God; for "He," says Jehovah, "shall come forth to me." Who sent Him, then? The answer is, His Father.

DAY 15
MORNING

*"That holy thing which shall be born of you shall be
called the Son of God."*
—Luke 1:35

Christ's humanity was perfectly holy. Upon this doctrine, you are well established; but you may well wonder that Jesus was always holy. He is conceived of a woman, and yet, no sort of sin comes from His birth. He is educated in the midst of sinful persons. It could not be otherwise, for there were none on earth who could be called good—all having become unprofitable—and although residing in the midst of sinners, in Him is no taint or trace of sin! He goes into the world, and as a physician must mingle with the sick, so He is found in the very worst of society. The harlot may speak to Him, and from the publican He turns not away, yet, from none of these did He receive any corrupt influence. He is tempted, and it is usually supposed that a man can scarcely be tempted; even should he overcome the temptation, without receiving some injury to his innocence. But the prince of this world came and had nothing in Christ; his fiery darts fell upon the nature of Christ as upon water, and were quenched at once. Satan was but as one who should whip the sea; he left no mark upon the perfect holiness of Christ. Imputation of sin would be the nearest approach to making our Lord a sinner; but let it always be remembered that, though Jehovah made Him to be sin for us, yet, He knew no sin. The world's sin was put upon the shoulders of Christ, and yet, He had no sin for all that…. The great Redeemer stood perfect, pure, spotless; and even in the conflict, when all the powers of hell were let loose against Him, and when God Himself had withdrawn—that withdrawal of God from us would have hardened our hearts—but it did not harden His heart. The taking away of God's grace from us is the ruin of our graces; but He had a wellspring of divine grace within Himself, and His purity lived on when God had withdrawn from Him. From the first dawn of His humanity in the womb to the time when He is laid in the new tomb, He is holy.

DAY 15

EVENING

"…full of grace and truth."
—John 1:14

Our God is not far from any one of His people this day. We are drawn nigh by the blood of Christ. God is everywhere present, but there is a higher presence of effectual grace in the person of the only begotten. Do not let us feel as if we worshiped a far-off God. Let us not repine as if we were deserted. Let us not feel alone, for the Father is with us. God is near you, therefore cheer the sad soul. Open your window towards Jerusalem, as Daniel did; pray, with your eye upon Christ, in whom all the fullness of the Godhead embodies the greatest nearness to us. God is never far away since Christ has come to dwell among men…. Let us come to Christ without fear, for He has grace to give, and He will give it to us abundantly whenever we need it. I like to think of the wording of my text. Leave out the parentheses, and it runs, "He dwelt among us full of grace." (See John 1:14.) He could not have dwelt among such provoking ones if He had not been full of grace. But if He dwells among us full of grace, we need not fear that He will cast us away because of our sins and failings. I invite you, therefore, to come boldly to Him who is full of forgiving love…. Don't we tell the sinner that God is not be sought for as far away, but that He is waiting to be gracious? Must I tell the believer the same? You may at this moment obtain all the grace you need. The door is open; enter and take what you will. Do not stop till you reach home and go through a set of religious exercises; but here, and now, believe in Jesus to the full. In the center of the camp is the incarnate God; Israel had but to go the central tent to find present help in time of trouble. In the person of Christ, who has said, *"I am with you always, even to the end of the world"* (Matthew 28:20), there is, in truth, all the grace you can possibly need. Come to this well and drink. Receive of His fullness, and go on your way rejoicing.

_____

_____

_____

_____

_____

_____

MORNING

"My soul does magnify the Lord."
—Luke 1:46

Mary knew that with God all things are possible, she had His promise delivered by an angel, and this was enough for her; on the strength of the Word which came forth from God, her heart leaped with pleasure and her tongue glorified His name. When I consider what it is which she believed, and how unhesitatingly she received the word, I am ready to give her, as a woman, a place almost as high as that which Abraham occupied as a man! And if I dare not call her the mother of the faithful, at least let her have due honor, as one of the most excellent of the mothers in Israel. The benediction of Elizabeth, Mary right well deserved, *"Blessed is she that believed"* (Luke 1:45). To her the *"substance of things hoped for"* was her faith, and that was also her *"evidence of things not seen"* (Hebrew 11:1). She knew, by the revelation of God, that she was to bear the promised Seed who would bruise the Serpent's head; but she had no other proof. This day there are those among us who have little or no conscious enjoyment of the Savior's presence; they walk in darkness and see no light; they are groaning over inbred sin, and mourning because corruptions prevail; let them now trust in the Lord, and remember that if they believe in the Son of God, Christ Jesus is within them; and by faith they may right gloriously chant the hallelujah of adoring love. Even though the sun gleams not forth today, the clouds and mists do not quench His light, and even though the Sun of Righteousness shines not on you at this instant, yet He keeps His place in yonder skies, and knows no variableness, neither shadow of a turning. If with all your digging, the well springs not up, yet there abides a constant fullness in that deep which crouches beneath in the heart and purpose of a God of love. What, if like David, you are much cast down, yet like he you can say to your soul, *"Hope you in God: for I shall yet praise Him, who is the health of my countenance"* (Psalm 42:11). Be glad then with Mary's joy—it is the joy of a Savior completely hers—but evidenced to be so, not by sense, but by faith.

DAY 16

EVENING

"My spirit has rejoiced in God my Savior."
—Luke 1:47

This is a season when all men expect us to be joyous. We compliment each other with the desire that we may have a "Merry Christmas." Some Christians, who are a little squeamish, do not like the word "merry." It is a right good Old Saxon word, having the joy of childhood, and the mirth of manhood in it; it brings before one's mind the old song of the midnight peal of bells, the holly, and the blazing log. I love it for its place in that most tender of all parables, where it is written, that, when the long-lost prodigal returned to his father safe and sound, *"They began to be merry"* (Luke 15:24). This is the season when we are expected to be happy; and my heart's desire is that in the highest and best sense, you who are believers may be "merry." Mary's heart was merry within her; but here was the mark of her joy—it was all holy merriment, it was every drop of it sacred mirth. It was not such merriment as worldlings will revel in today and tomorrow, but such merriment as the angels have around the throne of God, where they sing, *"Glory to God in the highest,"* while we sing, *"On earth peace, good will towards men"* (Luke 2:14). Such merry hearts have a continual feast. I want you, you children of the bride-chamber, to possess today and tomorrow, yes, all your days, the high and consecrated bliss of Mary, that you may not only read her words, but use them for yourselves, always experiencing their meaning…. In truth, moaning and pining is not the appointed way for worshipping God. We should take Mary as a pattern. All the year round I recommend her as an example to fainthearted and troubled ones. *"My spirit has rejoiced in God my Savior."* Cease from rejoicing in sensual things, and with sinful pleasures have no fellowship—for all such rejoicing is evil—but you cannot rejoice too much in the Lord!

_____

_____

_____

_____

_____

_____

MORNING

"Fear not: for, behold,
I bring you good tidings of great joy."
—Luke 2:10

The birth of Christ was the incarnation of God—it was God taking upon Himself human nature—a mystery, a wondrous mystery, to be believed in rather than to be defined! Yet so it was that in the manger lay an infant who was also infinite! A feeble child who was also the Creator of heaven and earth! How this could be we do not know but that it was so we assuredly believe, and therein do we rejoice! If God thus takes upon Himself human nature, then manhood is not abandoned nor given up as hopeless! When manhood had broken the bonds of the covenant and snatched from the one reserved tree the forbidden fruit, God might have said, "I give you up, O Adam, and cast off your race. Even as I gave up Lucifer and his entire host, so I abandon you to follow your own chosen course of rebellion!" But we have now no fear that the Lord has done this, for God has espoused manhood and taken it into union with Himself! Now manhood is not put aside by the Lord as an utterly accursed thing, to be an abomination to Him forever, for Jesus, the Well-beloved, is born of a virgin! God would not have taken manhood into union with Himself if He had not said, "Destroy it not, for a blessing is in it." I know the curse has fallen upon men because they have sinned, but evidently not on manhood in the abstract, for else had not Christ come to take upon Himself the form of man, and to be born of woman! The word made flesh means hope for manhood, notwithstanding the fall! The race is not to be outlawed and marked with the brand of death and hell, or to be utterly abandoned to destruction, for, lo, the Lord has married into the race and the Son of God has become the Son of Man! This is enough to make all that is within us sing for joy!

DAY 17

EVENING

"…which shall be to all people."
—Luke 2:10

I was very heavy yesterday in spirit, for this dreary weather tends greatly to depress the mind— "No lark could pipe to skies so dull and gray." But a thought struck me and filled me with intense joy. I tell it to you, not because it will seem anything to you, but as having gladdened myself. It is a bit all for myself to be placed in a parenthesis! It is this, that the joy of the birth of Christ in part belongs to those who tell of it, for the angels who proclaimed it were exceedingly glad, as glad as glad could be! I thought of this and whispered to my heart, "As I shall tell of Jesus born on earth for men, I will take license to be glad also; glad if for nothing else that I have such a message to bring to them." The tears stood in my eyes and stand there even now, to think that I should be privileged to say to my fellow men, "God has condescended to assume your nature that He might save you." These are as glad and as grand words as he of the golden mouth could have spoken. As for Cicero and Demosthenes, those eloquent orators had no such theme to dwell upon! Oh, joy, joy, joy! There was born into this world a man who is also God! My heart dances as David danced before the ark of God! This joy was meant, not for the tellers of the news alone, but for all who heard it. The glad tidings *"shall be to all people."* Read, "All the people," if you like, for so, perhaps, the letter of the original might demand. Well, then, it meant that it was joy to all the nation of the Jews—but assuredly our version is truer to the inner spirit of the text—it is joy to all people upon the face of the earth that Christ is born! There is not a nation under heaven but what has a right to be glad because God has come down among men! Sing together, you waste places of Jerusalem! … Exult and magnify Jehovah that His Son, His Only-Begotten, is also brother to mankind!

MORNING

"Glory to God in the highest."
—Luke 2:14.

Salvation is God's highest glory. He is glorified in every dewdrop that twinkles to the morning sun. He is magnified in every wood flower that blossoms in the copse, although it live to blush unseen, and waste its sweetness in the forest air. God is glorified in every bird that warbles on the spray; in every lamb that skips the mead. Do not the fishes in the sea praise Him? From the tiny minnow to the huge Leviathan, do not all creatures that swim the water bless and praise His name? Do not all created things extol Him? Is there anything beneath the sky, save man, that does not glorify God? Do not the stars exalt Him, when they write His name upon the azure of heaven in their golden letters? Do not the lightnings adore Him when they flash His brightness in arrows of light piercing the midnight darkness? Do not thunders extol Him when they roll like drums in the march of the God of armies? Do not all things exalt Him, from the least even to the greatest? But sing, sing, oh universe, till you have exhausted yourself, you cannot afford a song as sweet as the song of incarnation. Though creation may be a majestic organ of praise, it cannot reach the compass of the golden canticle—incarnation! There is more in that than in creation, more melody in Jesus in the manger, than there is in worlds on worlds rolling their grandeur round the throne of the Most High. Pause Christian, and consider this a minute. See how every attribute is here magnified. Lo! what wisdom is here. God becomes man that God may be just, and the justifier of the ungodly. Lo! what power, for where is power so great as when it conceals power? What power, that Godhead should unrobe itself and become man! Behold, what love is thus revealed to us when Jesus becomes a man…. The whole of God is glorified in Christ; and though some part of the name of God is written in the universe, it is here best read—in Him who was the Son of Man, and, yet, the Son of God.

EVENING

"And on earth peace, good will toward men."
—Luke 2:14.

It is superstitious to worship angels; it is but proper to love them. Although it would be a high sin, and an act of misdemeanor against the Sovereign Court of Heaven to pay the slightest adoration to the mightiest angel, yet it would be unkind and unseemly, if we did not give to holy angels a place in our heart's warmest love. In fact, he that contemplates the character of angels, and marks their many deeds of sympathy with men, and kindness towards them, cannot resist the impulse of his nature—the impulse of love towards them. The one incident in angelic history, to which our text refers, is enough to weld our hearts to them forever. How free from envy the angels were! Christ did not come from heaven to save their compeers when they fell. When Satan, the mighty angel, dragged with him a third part of the stars of heaven, Christ did not stoop from His throne to die for them; but He left them to be reserved in chains and darkness until the last great day. Yet angels did not envy men. Though they remembered that He took not up angels, yet they did not murmur when He took up the seed of Abraham; and though the blessed Master had never condescended to take the angel's form, they did not think it beneath them to express their joy when they found Him arrayed in the body of an infant. How free, too, they were from pride! They were not ashamed to come and tell the news to humble shepherds. Methinks they had as much joy in pouring out their songs that night before the shepherds, who were watching with their flocks, as they would have had if they had been commanded by their Master to sing their hymn in the halls of Caesar. Mere men—men possessed with pride, think it a fine thing to preach before kings and princes; and think it great condescension now and then to have to minister to the humble crowd. Not so the angels. They stretched their willing wings, and gladly sped from their bright seats above, to tell the shepherds on the plain by night, the marvelous story of an incarnate God.

DAY 19

MORNING

"You shall call His name Jesus."
—Matthew 1:21

Our Lord has other names of office and relationship, but "Jesus" is specially and peculiarly His own personal name and it is the Father who has thus named Him. Rest assured, therefore, that it is the best name that He could bear. God would not have given Him a name of secondary value, or about which there would be a trace of dishonor. The name is the highest, brightest, and noblest of names. It is the glory of our Lord to be a Savior. To the best that was ever born of woman, God has given the best name that any son of man could bear. JESUS is the most appropriate name that our Lord could receive. Of this we are quite certain, for the Father knew all about Him and could name Him well. He knows much more about the Lord Christ than all saints and angels put together, for *"No man knows the Son, but the Father"* (Matthew 11:27). To perfection the Father knew Him and He names Him Jesus. We may be sure, then, that our Lord is most of all a Savior and is best described by that term. God, the Father, who knows Him best, sees this to be His grand characteristic, that He is a Savior and is best represented by the name, "Jesus." Since infinite wisdom has selected it, we may be sure that it is a name which must be true, and must be verified by facts of no mean order. God, who cannot be mistaken, calls Him Jesus, a Savior, and therefore Jesus, a Savior He must be upon a grand scale, continually, abundantly, and in a most apparent manner. Neither will God refuse to accept the work which He has done, since by the gift of that name He has commissioned Him to save sinners. When we plead the name of Jesus before God, we bring Him back His own Word and appeal to Him by His own act and deed. Is not the name of Jesus to be viewed with reverential delight by each one of us, when we remember from where it came? He is not a Savior of our own setting up, but God the everlasting Father has set Him forth for our Deliverer and Savior.

DAY 19

EVENING

"For He shall save His people from their sins."
—Matthew 1:21

Notice yet again, the very gracious, but startling fact that our Lord's connection with His people lies in the direction of their sins. This is amazing condescension. He is called Savior in connection with His people, but it is in reference to their sins, because it is from their sins that they need to be saved. If they had never sinned, they would never have required a Savior, and there would have been no name of Jesus known on earth. That is a wonderful text—did you ever meditate upon it?—*"Who gave Himself for our sins"* (Galatians 1:4). As Martin Luther says, He never gave Himself for our righteousness, but He did give Himself for our sins. Sin is a horrible evil, a deadly poison, yet it is this which gives Jesus His title when He overcomes it. What a wonder to think upon! The first link between my soul and Christ is, not my goodness, but my badness; not my merit, but my misery; not my standing, but my falling; not my riches, but my need. He comes to visit His people, yet not to admire their beauties, but to remove their deformities; not to reward their virtues, but to forgive their sins. O you sinners, I mean real sinners, not you that call yourselves so because you are told you are such, but you who feel yourselves to be guilty before God, here is good news for you. O you self-condemned sinners, who feel that if you ever get salvation, Jesus must bring it to you and be the beginning and the end of it, I pray you rejoice in this dear, this precious, this blessed name, for Jesus has come to save you, even you. Go to Him as sinners, call Him, "Jesus," and cry, "O Lord Jesus, be Jesus to me, for I need Your salvation." Doubt not that He will fulfill His own name and exhibit His power in you. Only confess to Him your sin and He will save you from it. Only believe in Him and He will be your salvation.... He is nothing if He is not a Savior. He is anointed to this very end. His very name is a sham if He does not save His people from their sins.

MORNING

"To make ready a people prepared for the Lord."
—Luke 1:17

If we came and preached to men the necessity of preparation through so many weeks of fasting during a long Lent, or through so many days of scourging and penitence, they would attend to us at once, for they would be willing enough to make any preparation of that kind! But, when we say to them, "Come just as you are, with nothing in your hands to buy the mercy of God, with nothing wherewith to demand or to deserve it," men want a great deal of preparing before they will come to that point! Only the grace of God, working mightily through the Word, by the Spirit, will prepare men to come to Christ; prepared by being unprepared so far as any fitness of their own is concerned…. But John led his hearers on further than that, for they began to expect something as well as to hope for it. They expected that the Christ would speedily come and they expected some great blessings through the coming of the Messiah. And oh, when men, after hearing the gospel, have great expectations concerning God and His salvation, surely their expectations will not be long disappointed! ... When people come really expecting a blessing, they will be sure to get it! I believe that some folk go to hear ministers with the idea that there will be something to find fault with and, of course, they find that it is so. And when people come to hear another preacher, with the hope and expectation that God will bless them, of course God does bless them. Their expectation is divinely fulfilled! I always have a bright hope that a man will lay hold on Christ when he begins to expect to be saved, for he feels, then, that the time has come for him to find eternal life. John made ready *"a people prepared for the Lord"* because, first, he led them to thought. Next, he led them to hope, and then he led them to expectation; and this is a high measure of preparation!

DAY 20

EVENING

"He has regarded the low estate of His handmaiden."
—Luke 1:48

The long-expected Messiah is about to appear. He, for whom prophets and princes waited long, is now about to come—to be born of the Virgin of Nazareth. Truly there was never a subject of sweeter song than this—the stooping down of Godhead to the feebleness of manhood! When God manifested His power in the works of His hands, the morning stars sang together, and the sons of God shouted for joy; but when God manifests Himself, what music shall suffice for the grand psalm of adoring wonder? When wisdom and power are seen, these are but attributes; but in the incarnation it is the divine person which is revealed wrapped in a veil of our inferior clay— well might Mary sing, when earth and heaven even now are wondering at the condescending grace! Worthy of peerless music is the fact that, *"The Word was made flesh and dwelt among us"* (John 1:14).... We can no more think that God sits on high, indifferent to the needs and woes of men—for God has visited us, and come down to the lowliness of our estate. We no longer need bemoan that we can never participate in the moral glory and purity of God, for if God in glory can come down to His sinful creature, it is certainly less difficult to bear that creature, blood-washed and purified, up that starry way, that the redeemed one may sit down forever on His throne. Let us dream no longer in somber sadness that we cannot draw near to God so that He will really hear our prayers and pity our necessities, seeing that Jesus has become bone of our bone, and flesh of our flesh! He was born a baby as we are born, living a man as we must live, bearing the same infirmities and sorrows, and bowing His head to the same death.... The manger of Bethlehem was big with God's glory; in the incarnation was wrapped up all the blessedness by which a soul, snatched from the depths of sin, is lifted up to the heights of glory. Shall not our clearer knowledge lead us to heights of song which angelic guesses could not reach?

DAY 21
MORNING

"For to you is born this day in the city of David...."
—Luke 2:11

The Eternal seems to be so far away from us. He is infinite, and we are such little creatures. There appears to be a great gulf fixed between man and God, even on the ground of creatureship. But observe, He who is God has also become man. We never heard that God took the nature of angels into union with Himself; we may therefore say that between Godhead and angelhood there must be an infinite distance still; but here the Lord has actually taken manhood into union with Himself; there is therefore no longer a great gulf fixed, on the contrary, here is a marvelous union.... Our Lord Jesus Christ is in some senses more man than Adam. Adam was not born; Adam never had to struggle through the risks and weaknesses of infancy; he knew not the littlenesses of childhood—he was full grown at once. Father Adam could not sympathize with me as a baby and a child. But how manlike is Jesus! He is cradled with us in the manger; He does not begin with us in mid-life, as Adam, but He accompanies us in the pains and feebleness and infirmities of infancy, and He continues with us even to the grave. Beloved, this is such sweet comfort. He who is God this day was once an infant, so that if my cares are little and even trivial and comparatively infantile, I may go to Him, for He was once a Child. Though the great ones of the earth may sneer at the child of poverty, and say, "You are too mean, and your trouble is too slight for pity," I remember with humble joy that the King of heaven did hang upon a woman's breast, and was wrapped in swaddling bands, and therefore I tell Him all my griefs. How wonderful that He should have been an infant, and yet should be God over all, blessed forever! I am no longer afraid of God; this blessed link between me and God, the holy child Jesus, has taken all fear away.

EVENING

"…a Savior, which is Christ the Lord."
—Luke 2:11

It is evermore a joyous fact that God should be in alliance with man, especially when the alliance is so near that God should in very deed take our manhood into union with His godhead; so that God and man should constitute one divine, mysterious person. Sin had separated between God and man; but the incarnation bridges the separation: it is a prelude to the atoning sacrifice, but it is a prelude full of the richest hope. From henceforth, when God looks upon man, He will remember that His own Son is a man. From this day forth, when He beholds the sinner, if His wrath should burn, He will remember that His own Son, as man, stood in the sinner's place, and bore the sinner's doom. As in the case of war, the feud is ended when the opposing parties intermarry, so there is no more war between God and man, because God has taken man into intimate union with Himself. Herein, then, there was cause for joy. But there was more than that, for the shepherds were aware that *there had been promises made of old* which had been the hope and comfort of believers in all ages, and these *were now to be fulfilled.* There was that ancient promise made on the threshold of Eden to the first sinners of our race, that the Seed of the woman should bruise the Serpent's head; another promise made to the Father of the faithful that in his seed should all the nations of the earth be blessed, and promises uttered by the mouths of prophets and of saints since the world began. Now, the announcement of the angel of the Lord to the shepherds was a declaration that the covenant was fulfilled, that now in the fullness of time God would redeem His word, and the Messiah, who was to be Israel's glory and the world's hope; was now really come. Be glad you heavens, and be joyful O earth, for the Lord has done it, and in mercy has He visited His people. The Lord has not suffered His word to fail, but has fulfilled to His people His promises.

DAY 22

MORNING

*"And in this mountain shall the L*ORD *of hosts*
make to all people a feast of fat things,
a feast of wines on the lees, of fat things full of marrow,
of wines on the lees well refined."
—Isaiah 25:6

On Christmas-day we shall find all the world enjoying themselves with all the good cheer which they can afford. Servants of God, you who have the largest share in the person of Him who was born at Bethlehem, I invite you to the best of all Christmas fare—to nobler food than makes the table groan—bread from heaven, food for your spirit. Behold, how rich and how abundant are the provisions which God has made for the high festival which He would have His servants keep, not now and then, but all the days of their lives! ... It is described as consisting of viands of the best, nay, of the best of the best. They are fat things, but they are also fat things full of marrow. Wines are provided of the most delicious and invigorating kind, wines on the lees, which retain their aroma, their strength, and their flavor; but these are most ancient and rare, having been so long kept that they have become well refined; by long standing they have purified, clarified themselves, and brought themselves to the highest degree of brightness and excellence. The best of the best God has provided in the gospel for the sons of men. Let us attentively survey the blessings of the gospel, and observe that they are fat things, and fat things full of marrow. One of the first gospel blessings is that of complete justification. A sinner, though guilty in himself, no sooner believes in Jesus than all his sins are pardoned. The righteousness of Christ becomes his righteousness, and he is accepted in the Beloved. Now, this is a delicious dish indeed. Here is something for the soul to feed upon. To think that I, though a deeply guilty one, am absolved of God, and set free from the bondage of the law! ... Beloved, this is such a precious truth, that when the soul feeds on it, it experiences a quiet peace, a deep and heavenly calm, to be found nowhere on earth besides.

DAY 22

EVENING

"And this shall be a sign to you; You shall find the
babe wrapped in swaddling clothes, lying in a manger."
—Luke 2:12

The sign that the joy of the world had come was this—
they were to go to the manger to find the Christ in it, and
He was to be the sign. Every circumstance is therefore
instructive. The babe was found *"wrapped in swaddling*
clothes." Now, observe, as you look at this infant, that there
is not the remotest appearance of *temporal power* here.
Mark the two little puny arms of a little babe that must be
carried if it go. Alas, the nations of the earth look for joy in
military power…. What pride flushes the patriot's cheek
when he remembers that his nation can murder faster
than any other people. Ah, foolish generation, you are
groping in the flames of hell to find your heaven, raking
amid blood and bones for the foul thing which you call
glory. A nation's joy can never lie in the misery of others.
Killing is not the path to prosperity; huge armaments are a
curse to the nation itself as well as to its neighbors. The joy
of a nation is a golden sand over which no stream of blood
has ever rippled. It is only found in that river, the streams

whereof make glad the city of God. (See Psalm 46:4.) The weakness of submissive gentleness is true power. Jesus founds His eternal empire not on force but on love. Here, O you people, see your hope; the mild pacific Prince, whose glory is His self-sacrifice, is our true benefactor. But look again, and you shall observe *no pomp* to dazzle you. Is the Child wrapped in purple and fine linen? Ah, no. Sleeps He in a cradle of gold? The manger alone is His shelter. No crown is upon the babe's head, neither does a coronet surround the mother's brow. A simple maiden of Galilee, and a little child in ordinary swaddling bands, it is all you see…. Vain are the men who look for joy in pomp; it lies in truth and righteousness, in peace and salvation, of which yonder newborn Prince in the garments of a peasant child is the true symbol.

DAY 23

MORNING

"You have left your first love."
—Revelation 2:4

Every season has its own proper fruit—apples for autumn, holly berries for Christmas. The earth brings forth according to the period of the year, and with man there is a time for every purpose under heaven. At this season the world is engaged in congratulating itself, and in expressing its complimentary wishes for the good of its citizens; let me suggest extra and more solid work for Christians. As we think, today, of the birth of the Savior, let us aspire after a fresh birth of the Savior in our hearts— that as He is already "formed in us the hope of glory" (see Colossians 1:27) we may be "renewed in the spirit of our minds" (see Ephesians 4:23)—that we may go again to the Bethlehem of our spiritual nativity, and do our first works, enjoy our first loves, and feast with Jesus as we did in the holy, happy, heavenly days of our espousals. Let us go to Jesus with something of that youthful freshness and excessive delight which was so manifest in us when we looked to Him at first. Let Him be crowned anew by us, for He is still adorned with the dew of His youth, and remains "The same yesterday, today and forever." (See Hebrews 13:8.) The citizens of Durham, though they dwell not far from the Scotch border, and consequently, in the olden times, were frequently liable to be attacked, were exempted from the toils of war because there was a cathedral within their walls, and they were set aside to the bishop's service, being called in the olden times by the name of "holy work-folk." Now, we citizens of the New Jerusalem, having the Lord Jesus in our midst, may well excuse ourselves from the ordinary ways of celebrating this season; and considering ourselves to be "holy work-folk," we may keep it, after a different sort from other men, in holy contemplation, and in blessed service of that gracious God whose unspeakable gift to us is the newborn King.

DAY 23

EVENING

"She gave birth to her firstborn, a son. She wrapped him in cloths and placed him in a manger, because there was no room for them in the inn."
—Luke 2:7

As the palace, and the forum, and the inn have no room for Christ, and as the places of public resort have none, have you room for Christ? "Well," says one, "I have room for Him, but I am not worthy that He should come to me." Ah, I did not ask about worthiness! Have you room for Him? "Oh," says one, "I have an empty void the world can never fill!" Ah, I see you do have room for Him. "Oh, but the room I have in my heart is so base!" So was the manger! "But it is so despicable!" So was the manger a thing to be despised! "Ah, but my heart is so foul!" So, perhaps, the manger may have been! "Oh, but I feel it is a place not at all fit for Christ!" Nor was the manger a place fit for Him, and yet there He was laid. "Oh, but I have been such a sinner; I feel as if my heart had been a den of beasts and devils!" Well, the manger had been a place where beasts had fed. Have you room for Him? Never mind what the past has been; He can forget and forgive. It matters not what even the present state may be if you mourn it! If you have but room for Christ, He will come and be your guest.... Here is my royal Master—have you room for Him? Here is the Son of God made flesh—have you room for Him? Here is He who can forgive all sin—have you room for Him? Here is He who can take you up out of the horrible pit of hell, and out of the miry clay—have you room for Him? Here is He who, when He comes in will never go out again but abide with you forever to make your heart a heaven of joy and bliss for you—have you room for Him? It is all I ask. Your emptiness, your nothingness, your need of feeling, your need of goodness, your need of grace—all these will be but room for Him! Have you room for Him?

MORNING

"How sweet are Your words to my taste!
Yea, sweeter than honey to my mouth!"
—Psalm 119:103

This is a time of feasting and we may as well have our feast as other people have theirs. Let us see whether there is not something for our spiritual palate, something to satisfy our spiritual appetite that we may eat, and be content, and rejoice before the Lord. Do you not think that two of the words in our text are very strange? If you had written them, would you not have said, "How sweet are Your words unto my ears"? The psalmist says, *"How sweet are Your words to my palate!"* for that is the word in the margin. He did not write, "Yes, sweeter than honey to my hearing!" but, "sweeter than honey to my mouth!" Are words, then, things that we can taste and eat? No, not if they are the words of man—it would take many of our words to fill a hungry belly. "Be you warmed and filled." It would take many tons of that sort of fodder to feed "a brother or sister destitute of daily food," for man's words are air and airy, light and frothy. They often deceive, they mock, and they awaken hopes which are never realized. But God's words are full of substance—they are spirit, they are life, they are to be fed upon by the spiritually hungry! Marvel not that I say this to you! It was God's Word that made us—is it any wonder that His Word should sustain us? If His Word gives life, do you wonder that His Word should also give food for that life? Marvel not, for it is written—*"Man shall not live by bread, alone, but by every word that proceeds out of the mouth of God"* (Matthew 4:4). God's words are meat, drink and food—and if bodies live not upon words—souls and spirits feed upon the Words of God, and so are satisfied and full of delight! ... I love this thought of tasting God's word because it implies nearness, an actual reception and a veritable holding-fast of that which is so appreciated by the taste.

DAY 24

EVENING

*"And when they had seen it, they made known abroad
the saying which was told them concerning this Child."*
—Luke 2:17

Though the shepherds told what they heard from
heaven, remember that they spoke of what they had seen
below. They had, by observation, made those truths of
God most surely their own which had first been spoken
to them by revelation. No man can speak of the things of
God with any success until the doctrine which he finds in
the Bible, he finds also in his heart. We must bring down
the mystery and make it plain, by knowing, by the teaching of the Holy Spirit, its practical power on the heart
and conscience. My brethren, the gospel which we preach
is most surely revealed to us by the Lord; but, moreover,
our hearts have tried and proved, have grasped, have felt,
and have realized its truth and power. If we have not been
able to understand its heights and depths, yet we have felt
its mystic power upon our heart and spirit. It has plainly
revealed sin to us; it has revealed to us our pardon. It has
killed the reigning power of sin; it has given us Christ to
reign over us, and the Holy Spirit to dwell within our

bodies as in a temple. Now we must speak. I do not urge any of you to speak of Jesus, who merely know the word as you find it in the Bible, as your teaching can have but little power; but I do speak earnestly to you who know its mighty influence upon the heart, who have not only heard of the Baby, but have seen Him in the manger, taken Him up in your own arms and received Him as being born to you, a Savior to you, *Christos*, the Anointed for you, Jesus the Savior from sin, for you. Beloved, can you do otherwise than speak of the things which you have seen and heard? God has made you to taste and to handle of this good word of life, and you must not, you dare not hold your peace, but you must tell friends and neighbors what you have felt within.

MORNING

"Where is He that is born King of the Jews?"
—Matthew 2:2

The King of the Jews was born, but Herod did not ask, "Where is He?" until his jealousy was excited, and then he asked the question in a malicious spirit. Christ was born at Bethlehem, near Jerusalem; yet throughout all the streets of the holy city there were no inquirers, "Where is He?" He was to be the glory of Israel, and yet in Israel there were few indeed, who, like these wise men, asked the question, "Where is He?"… He is despised and rejected of men; men see in Him no beauty that they should desire Him, but there are a chosen number who inquire diligently, and who come to receive Him; to these He gives power to become the sons of God! A happy circumstance it is, therefore, when there is interest shown; interest is not always demonstrated in the things of Christ, even by our regular hearers; it gets to be a mere mechanical habit to attend public worship; you become accustomed to sit through such a part of the service, to stand and sing at such another time, and to listen to the preacher with an apparent attention during the sermon, but to be really interested, to long to know what it is all about—to know especially whether you have a part in it, whether Jesus came from heaven to save you; whether for you He was born of the virgin—to make such personal inquiries with deep anxiety is far from being a general practice. Would God that all who have ears to hear would hear in truth! Wherever the word is heard with solemn interest, it is a very encouraging sign; it was said of old, "They shall ask the way to Zion with their faces toward it." (See Jeremiah 50:5.) When a man listens with deep attention to the word of God, searches God's book, and engages in thoughtful meditation with the view of understanding the gospel, we have much hope for him!

EVENING

"For we have seen His star in the east,
and are come to worship Him."
—Matthew 2:2

The wise men did not regard the favor of seeing the star as a matter to be rested in; they did not say, "We have seen His star, and that is enough." Many say, "Well, we attend a place of worship regularly; is not that enough?" There are those who say, "We were baptized; baptism brought regeneration with it; we come to the sacrament, and do we not get grace through it?" Poor souls! The star which leads to Christ they mistake for Christ Himself, and worship the star instead of the Lord! O may none of you ever be so foolish as to rest in outward ordinances! ... No, beloved, we desire to worship the Most High in all simplicity and earnestness of spirit, and never to stop in the outward form, lest we are foolish enough to think that to see the star is sufficient, and therefore fail to find the incarnate God. Note well that these wise men did not find satisfaction in what they had themselves done to reach the child. As we have observed, they may have come hundreds of miles, but they did not mention it; they did not sit down and say, "Well, we have journeyed across deserts, over hills, and across rivers; it is enough." No, they must find the newborn King, nothing else would satisfy them! Do not say, dear hearer, "I have been praying now for months; I have been searching the Scriptures for weeks to find the Savior." I am glad you have done so, but do not rest in it; you must get Christ, or else you will perish after all your exertion and your trouble! You need Jesus; nothing more than Jesus, but nothing less than Jesus; nor must you be satisfied with traveling in the way the star would lead you, you must reach HIM! Do not stop short of eternal life; lay hold on it, not merely seek it and long for it, but lay hold on eternal life, and do not be content until it is an ascertained fact with you that Jesus Christ is yours.

MORNING

*"And all they that heard it wondered at those things
which were told them by the shepherds."*
—Luke 2:18

Let me suggest to you that holy wonder at what God has done should be very natural to you.... Probably it is most marvelous to you in its relation to yourself, that you should be redeemed by blood; that God should forsake the thrones and royalties above to suffer shamefully below for you. If you know yourself, you can never see any adequate motive or reason in your own flesh for such a deed as this. "Why such love to me?" you will say. What should you and I say, if David, sitting in his house, could only say, "Who am I, O Lord God, and what is my house, that You have brought me up to now?" Had we been the most meritorious of individuals, and had unceasingly kept the Lord's commands, we could not have deserved such a priceless gift as incarnation! But, sinners, offenders who revolted and went from God further and further, what shall we say of this incarnate God dying for us, but, *"Herein is love, not that we loved God, but that He loved us"* (1 John 4:10). Let your soul lose itself in wonder, for wonder, dear friends, is in this way a very practical emotion. Holy wonder will lead you to grateful worship; being astonished at what God has done, you will pour out your soul with astonishment at the foot of the golden throne with the song, *"Blessing, and honor, and glory, and power, be to Him that sits upon the throne, and to the Lamb for ever and ever"* (Revelation 5:13). Filled with this wonder, it will cause you a godly watchfulness; you will be afraid to sin against such love as this! Feeling the presence of the mighty God in the gift of His dear Son, you will take off your shoes, because the place where you stand is holy ground. You will be moved at the same time to a glorious hope. If Jesus has given Himself to you, if He has done this marvelous thing on your behalf, you will feel that heaven itself is not too great for your expectation.

DAY 26

EVENING

"But Mary kept all these things,
and pondered them in her heart."
—Luke 2:19

There was an exercise on the part of this blessed woman, of the three great parts of her being; her memory—she kept all these things; her affections—she kept them in her heart; her intellect— she pondered them, considered them, weighed them, turned them over; so that memory, affection, and understanding, were all exercised about these things. We delight to see this in Mary, but we are not at all surprised when we recollect that she was, in some sense, the most concerned of all on earth—for it was of her that Jesus Christ had been born. Those who come nearest to Jesus, and enter the most closely into fellowship with Him, will be sure to be the most engrossed with Him. Certain persons are best esteemed at a distance, but not the Savior; when you shall have known Him to the very fullest, then shall you love Him with the love which passes knowledge; you shall comprehend the heights, and depths, and lengths, and breadths of His love. And when you shall do so, then your own love shall swell beyond all length and breadth, all height and depth. The birth most concerned Mary, and therefore, she was the most impressed with it. Note the way in which her concern was shown…we do not read so much of her telling abroad as pondering within. No doubt she had her circle and her word to speak in it; but for the most part she, like another Mary, sat still in the house…. The word, "ponder," as you know, means to weigh. Make ready the scales of judgment. Oh, but where are the scales that can weigh the Lord Christ? *"He takes up the isles as a very little thing"* (Isaiah 40:15)—who shall take Him up? *"He weighed the mountains in scales"* (Isaiah 40:12). In what scales shall we weigh Him? Be it so, if your understanding cannot comprehend, let your affections apprehend; and if your spirit cannot compass the Lord Jesus in the arms of its understanding, let it embrace Him in the arms of your affection. Oh, beloved, here is blessed Christmas work for you, if, like Mary, you lay up all these things in your heart and ponder upon them!

MORNING

*"Go home to your friends, and tell them how great
things the Lord has done for you,
and has had compassion on you."*
—Mark 5:19

I [wish to] send you home this Christmas Day to be missionaries in the localities to which you belong and to be real preachers! Dear friends, do tell this story when you go home.... First, tell it truthfully. Do not tell more than you know. Do not tell John Bunyan's experience, when you ought to tell your own! Do not tell your mother you have felt what only Rutherford felt.... In the next place, tell it very humbly. I have said that before. Do not intrude yourselves upon those who are older and know more, but tell your story humbly. Not as a preacher, not ex-cathedra but as a friend and as a son. Next, tell it very earnestly. Let them see you mean it. Do not talk about religion flippantly. You will do no good if you do. Do not make puns on texts. Do not quote Scripture by way of joke—if you do, you may talk till you are dumb—you will do no good if you in the least degree give them occasion to laugh by laughing at holy things yourself. Tell it very earnestly. And then, tell it very devoutly. Do not try to tell your tale to man till you have told it, first, to God. When you are at home on Christmas Day let no one see your face till God has seen it. Be up in the morning. Wrestle with God, and if your friends are not converted, wrestle with God for them—and then you will find it easy work to wrestle with them for God. Seek, if you can, to get them one by one and tell them the story. Do not be afraid—only think of the good you may possibly do, by God's grace. Remember, he that saves a soul from death has covered a multitude of sins and he shall have stars in his crown forever and ever. Seek to be under God—to be the means of leading your own beloved brothers and sisters to seek and to find the Lord Jesus Christ.

EVENING

*"They saw the young Child with Mary His mother,
and fell down, and worshiped Him: and when they
had opened their treasures, they presented to Him
gifts; gold, frankincense, and myrrh."*
—Matthew 2:11

After worshipping, the wise men presented their gifts. One broke open his case of gold, and laid it at the feet of the newborn King; another presented frankincense, one of the precious products of the country from which they came; and the other laid myrrh at the Redeemer's feet. All these they gave to prove the truth of their worship; they gave substantial offerings with no stingy hand. And now, after you have worshipped Christ in your soul, and seen Him with the eyes of faith, it will not be necessary that I should say to you, give Him yourself, give Him your heart, give Him your substance; why, you will not be able to help doing it! He who really loves the Savior in his heart cannot help devoting to Him his life, his strength, his all! With some people, when they give Christ anything, or do anything for Him, it is dreadfully forced work; they say, "The love of Christ ought to compel us." I do not know that there is any such text as that in the Bible, but I do remember one text that runs thus—"The love of Christ compels us." (See 2 Corinthians 5:14.) If it does not compel us, it is because it is not in us; it is not merely a thing which ought to be, it must be. If any man loves Christ, he will very soon find ways and means of proving his love by his sacrifices. Go home, Mary, and fetch the alabaster box, and pour the ointment on His head; and if any say, "Why this waste?" you will have a good reply; you have had much forgiven you, and therefore you love much. If you have gold, give it; if you have frankincense, give it; if you have myrrh, give it to Jesus. And if you have none of these things, give Him your love—all your love and that will be gold and spices all in one! Give Him your tongue, speak of Him! Give Him your hands, work for Him! Give Him your whole self; I know you will, for He loved you, and gave Himself for you.

MORNING

"Then took he Him up in his arms, and blessed God."
—Luke 2:28

Heaven and earth shall pass away, but if you trust Christ, you shall never be ashamed! There was never a man yet who dared trust Christ and yet found that Christ was not equal to his need, or that He did not fully supply all his needs. Simeon took Christ up in his arms. Somebody might have said, "Old man, what have you to do with the newborn King? Old man, you may be just and devout, but dare you handle the incarnate God? Dare you fondle Him upon whose shoulders God has laid the key of His kingdom, whose name is called Wonderful, Counselor, the Mighty God, the Everlasting Father, and the Prince of Peace? Dare you touch Him?" Yes, he dares do it! He takes Him up in his arms. He clasps Him to his heart. He rejoices over Him. He is ready to die with delight, now that he has found Christ! Come, poor troubled ones, come tonight and take Christ into your arms! And you, dear saints of God, who have done this long ago, do it again! Take Him right up into your arms, as though He were still a babe. Take Him to your heart and say, "He is everything to me; my love, my hope, my brother—this blessed incarnate God who loved me and gave Himself for me." If you can do this, it shall be well with you now, it shall be well with you in death, and it shall be well with you throughout eternity! ... See Christ, and what else is there to see? Now, whether you sail over the blue sea beneath a bluer sky, or dive into the deeps of this murky atmosphere; whether you are in a palace or in a dungeon, sick or full of bounding health; all these are items of small consequence if your eyes have seen God's salvation, for God has blessed you as only God can bless you! Go and live in peace and go and die in peace; and praise the name of Him who gave you such a Savior to see, and the power to see Him!

DAY 28

EVENING

"He shall be great."
—Luke 1:32

I was wishing that I had the tongues of men and of angels with which to set forth my theme tonight, and yet I shall retract my wish, for the subject is such, that if my words were the most common that could be found—yes, if they were ungrammatical, and if they were put together in a most uncouth manner, it would little matter, for failure awaits me in any case. The subject far transcends all utterance. Jesus is such a one that no oratory can ever reach the height of His glory, and the simplest words are best suited to a subject so sublime. Fine words would be but tawdry things to hang beside the unspeakably glorious Lord. I can say no more than that He is great. If I could tell forth His greatness with choral symphonies of cherubim, yet I would fail to reach the height of this great argument. I will be content if I can touch the hem of the garment of His greatness. If the Lord will but set us in a cleft of the rock, and only make us see the back parts of His character, we shall be overcome by the vision. As yet, even of Jesus, the face of His full glory cannot be seen, or if seen, it cannot be described. Were we caught up to the third heaven we should have little to say on coming back, for we would have seen things which were not lawful for us to utter. I shall not therefore fail with loss of honor if I tell you that my utmost success at this time will but touch the fringe of the splendor of the Son of Man. This is not the time of His clearest revealing. The day is coming for the manifestation of the Lord; as yet He shines not forth among men in His noontide. His Second Advent shall more fully reveal Him. Then shall His people *shine forth as the sun in the kingdom of their Father*" (Matthew 13:43), because He also shall rise in the clear face of heaven as the Sun of Righteousness, greatly blessing the sons of men.

_____

_____

_____

_____

_____

_____

ABOUT THE AUTHOR

Charles Haddon Spurgeon (1834–1892) was born on June 19, 1834, at Kelvedon, Essex, England, the firstborn of eight surviving children. His parents were committed Christians, and his father was a preacher. Spurgeon was converted in 1850 at the age of fifteen. He began to help the poor and to hand out tracts, and was known as "The Boy Preacher."

His next six years were eventful. He preached his first sermon at the age of sixteen. At age eighteen, he became the pastor of Waterbeach Baptist Chapel, preaching in a barn. Spurgeon preached over six hundred times before he reached the age of twenty. By 1854, he was well-known and was asked to become the pastor of New Park Street Chapel in London. In 1856, Spurgeon married Susannah Thompson; they had twin sons, both of whom later entered the ministry.

Spurgeon's compelling sermons and lively preaching style drew multitudes of people, and many came to Christ. Soon, the crowds had grown so large that they blocked the narrow streets near the church. Services eventually had to be held in rented halls, and he often preached to congregations of more than ten thousand. The Metropolitan

Tabernacle was built in 1861 to accommodate the large numbers of people.

Spurgeon published over two thousand sermons, which were so popular that they literally sold by the ton. At one point his sermons sold twenty-five thousand copies every week. An 1870 edition of the English magazine *Vanity Fair* called him an "original and powerful preacher…honest, resolute, sincere; lively, entertaining." He appealed constantly to his hearers to move on in the Christian faith, to allow the Lord to minister to them individually, and to be used of God to win the lost to Christ. His sermons were scripturally inspiring and highlighted with flashes of spontaneous and delightful humor. The prime minister of England, members of the royal family, and Florence Nightingale, among others, went to hear him preach. Spurgeon preached to an estimated ten million people throughout his life. Not surprisingly, he is called the "Prince of Preachers."

In addition to his powerful preaching, Spurgeon founded and supported charitable outreaches, including educational institutions. His pastors' college, which is still in existence today, taught nearly nine hundred students in Spurgeon's time. He also founded the famous Stockwell Orphanage.

In his later years, Spurgeon often publicly disagreed with the emergence of modern biblical criticism that led the believer away from a total dependence on the Word of God.

Charles Spurgeon died at Menton, France, in 1892, leaving a powerful legacy of writings for any believer who seeks to know the Lord Jesus more fully.

SOURCES

Day 1 Morning: From "The Waiting Church," http://biblehub.com/sermons/auth/spurgeon/the_waiting_church.htm (accessed June 21, 2017).

Day 1 Evening: From "Renewing Strength," Metropolitan Tabernacle, Newington, edited by Emmett O'Donnell, https://www.spurgeongems.org/vols28-30/chs1756.pdf (accessed June 21, 2017).

Day 2 Morning: From "Christ the Conqueror of Satan," November 26, 1876, Metropolitan Tabernacle, Newington, http://www.spurgeon.org/sermons/1326.php (accessed June 9, 2017).

Day 2 Evening: From "Christ the Conqueror of Satan," November 26, 1876, Metropolitan Tabernacle, Newington, http://www.spurgeon.org/sermons/1326.php (accessed June 9, 2017).

Day 3 Morning: From "Brave Waiting," August 26, 1877, Metropolitan Tabernacle, Newington, http://www.spurgeongems.org/vols22-24/chs1371.pdf (accessed June 21, 2017).

Day 3 Evening: From "Brave Waiting," August 26, 1877, Metropolitan Tabernacle, Newington, edited by Emmett O'Donnell, http://www.spurgeongems.org/vols22-24/chs1371.pdf (accessed June 21, 2017).

Day 4 Morning: From "Magnificat," http://biblehub.com/sermons/auth/spurgeon/magnificat.htm (accessed June 21, 2017).

Day 4 Evening: From "Waiting Only Upon God," August 2, 1857, Music Hall, Royal Surrey Gardens, http://biblehub.com/sermons/auth/spurgeon/waiting_only_upon_god.htm (accessed June 21, 2017).

Day 5 Morning: From "Immanuel—the Light of Life," September 14, 1890, Metropolitan Tabernacle, Newington, edited by Emmett O'Donnell, http://www.spurgeongems.org/vols34-36/chs2163.pdf (accessed June 22, 2017).

Day 5 Evening: From "Praying and Waiting," http://biblehub.com/sermons/auth/spurgeon/praying_and_waiting.htm (accessed June 21, 2017).

Day 6 Morning: From "The Tender Mercy of Our God," http://biblehub.com/sermons/auth/spurgeon/the_tender_mercy_of_our_god.htm (accessed June 21, 2017).

Day 6 Evening: From "Shiloh," http://biblehub.com/sermons/auth/spurgeon/shiloh.htm (accessed June 21, 2017).

Day 7 Morning: From "The Condescension of Christ," September 3, 1867, at Music Hall, Royal Surrey Gardens, http://biblehub.com/sermons/auth/spurgeon/the_condescension_of_christ.htm (accessed June 21, 2017).

Day 7 Evening: From "The Condescension of Christ," September 3, 1867, Music Hall, Royal Surrey Gardens, http://biblehub.com/sermons/auth/spurgeon/the_condescension_of_christ.htm (accessed June 21, 2017).

Day 8 Morning: From "The Hope of Future Bliss," May 20, 1855, at Exeter Hall, Strand, http://biblehub.com/sermons/auth/spurgeon/the_hope_of_future_bliss.htm (accessed June 21, 2017).

Day 8 Evening: From "Where Is the Lord?" May 29, 1892, Metropolitan Tabernacle, Newington, http://biblehub.com/library/spurgeon/spurgeons_sermons_volume_38_1892/where_is_the_lord.htm (accessed June 21, 2017).

Day 9 Morning: From "Jesus—All Blessing and All Blest," February 1, 1891, Metropolitan Tabernacle, Newington, http://biblehub.com/sermons/auth/spurgeon/jesus_--_all_blessing_and_all_blest.htm (accessed June 21, 2017).

Day 9 Evening: From "God With Us," December 26, 1875, Metropolitan Tabernacle, Newington, edited by Emmett O'Donnell, http://www.spurgeongems.org/vols19-21/chs1270.pdf (accessed June 21, 2017).

Day 10 Morning: From "Out of Egypt," August 20, 1882, Metropolitan Tabernacle, Newington, edited by Emmett O'Donnell, http://www.spurgeongems.org/vols28-30/chs1675.pdf (accessed June 21, 2017).

Day 10 Evening: From "Out of Egypt," August 20, 1882, Metropolitan Tabernacle, Newington, edited by Emmett O'Donnell, http://www.spurgeongems.org/vols28-30/chs1675.pdf (accessed June 21, 2017).

Day 11 Morning: From "Consolation in Christ," December 2, 1860, Metropolitan Tabernacle, Newington, edited by Emmett O'Donnell, http://www.spurgeongems.org/vols7-9/chs348.pdf (accessed June 21, 2017).

Day 11 Evening: From "Two Advents of Christ," December 22, 1861, Metropolitan Tabernacle, Newington, edited by Emmett O'Donnell, http://www.spurgeongems.org/vols7-9/chs430.pdf (accessed June 21, 2017).

Day 12 Morning: From "The Holy Child, Jesus," December 20, 1863, Metropolitan Tabernacle, Newington, edited by Emmett O'Donnell, http://www.spurgeongems.org/vols7-9/chs545.pdf (accessed June 21, 2017).

Day 12 Evening: From "The Holy Child, Jesus," December 20, 1863, Metropolitan Tabernacle, Newington, edited by Emmett O'Donnell, http://www.spurgeongems.org/vols7-9/chs545.pdf (accessed June 21, 2017).

Day 13 Morning: From "The Holy Child, Jesus," December 20, 1863, Metropolitan Tabernacle, Newington, edited by Emmett O'Donnell, http://www.spurgeongems.org/vols7-9/chs545.pdf (accessed June 21, 2017).

Day 13 Evening: From "Simeon," edited by Emmett O'Donnell, http://www.spurgeongems.org/vols10-12/chs659.pdf (accessed June 21, 2017).

Day 14 Morning: From "The Incarnation and Birth of Christ," December 23, 1855, New Park Street Chapel, Southwark, http://biblehub.com/sermons/auth/spurgeon/the_incarnation_and_birth_of_christ.htm (accessed June 21, 2017).

Day 14 Evening: From "The Incarnation and Birth of Christ," December 23, 1855, New Park Street Chapel, Southwark, http://biblehub.com/sermons/auth/spurgeon/the_incarnation_and_birth_of_christ.htm (accessed June 21, 2017).

Day 15 Morning: From "The Holy Child, Jesus," December 20, 1863, Metropolitan Tabernacle, Newington, edited by Emmett O'Donnell, http://www.spurgeongems.org/vols7-9/chs545.pdf (accessed June 21, 2017).

Day 15 Evening: From "The True Tabernacle," September 27, 1855, Metropolitan Tabernacle, Newington, http://www.spurgeon.org/sermons/1862.php (accessed June 9, 2017).

Day 16 Morning: From "Mary's Song," December 25, 1864, Metropolitan Tabernacle, Newington, edited by Emmett O'Donnell, http://www.spurgeongems.org/vols10-12/chs606.pdf (accessed June 21, 2017).

Day 16 Evening: From "Mary's Song," December 25, 1864, Metropolitan Tabernacle, Newington, edited by Emmett O'Donnell, http://www.spurgeongems.org/vols10-12/chs606.pdf (accessed June 21, 2017).

Day 17 Morning: From "The Great Birthday," December 24, 1876, Metropolitan Tabernacle, Newington, edited by Emmett O'Donnell, http://www.spurgeongems.org/vols22-24/chs1330.pdf (accessed June 21, 2017).

Day 17 Evening: From "The Great Birthday," December 24, 1876, Metropolitan Tabernacle, Newington, edited by Emmett O'Donnell, http://www.spurgeongems.org/vols22-24/chs1330.pdf (accessed June 21, 2017).

Day 18 Morning: From "The First Christmas Carol," December 20, 1857, Music Hall, Royal Surrey Gardens, http://www.spurgeon.org/sermons/0168.php (accessed June 9, 2017).

Day 18 Evening: From "The First Christmas Carol," December 20, 1857, Music Hall, Royal Surrey Gardens, http://www.spurgeon.org/sermons/0168.php (accessed June 9, 2017).

Day 19 Morning: From "Jesus!" September 15, 1878, Metropolitan Tabernacle, Newington, edited by Emmett O'Donnell, http://www.spurgeongems.org/vols22-24/chs1434.pdf (accessed June 21, 2017).

Day 19 Evening: From "Jesus!" September 15, 1878, Metropolitan Tabernacle, Newington, edited by Emmett O'Donnell, http://www.spurgeongems.org/vols22-24/chs1434.pdf (accessed June 21, 2017).

Day 20 Morning: From "A People Prepared for the Lord," March 17, 1895, Metropolitan Tabernacle, Newington, edited by Emmett O'Donnell, http://www.spurgeongems.org/vols40-42/chs2404.pdf (accessed June 21, 2017).

Day 20 Evening: From "Mary's Song," December 25, 1864, Metropolitan Tabernacle, Newington, edited by Emmett O'Donnell, http://www.spurgeongems.org/vols10-12/chs606.pdf (accessed June 21, 2017).

Day 21 Morning: From "God Incarnate, the End of Fear," December 23, 1866, Metropolitan Tabernacle, Newington, edited by Emmett O'Donnell, http://www.spurgeongems.org/vols10-12/chs727.pdf (accessed June 21, 2017).

Day 21 Evening: From "Joy Born at Bethlehem," December 24, 1871, Metropolitan Tabernacle, Newington, http://www.spurgeon.org/sermons/1026.php (accessed June 9, 2017).

Day 22 Morning: From Charles Spurgeon, "Good Cheer for Christmas," December 20, 1868, http://www.biblebb.com/files/spurgeon/goodchr.htm (accessed June 8, 2017).

Day 22 Evening: From "Joy Born at Bethlehem," December 24, 1871, Metropolitan Tabernacle, Newington, http://www.biblebb.com/files/spurgeon/1026.htm (accessed June 21, 2017).

Day 23 Morning: From "Holy Work for Christmas," December 24, 1865, Metropolitan Tabernacle, Newington, edited by Emmett O'Donnell, http://www.spurgeongems.org/vols10-12/chs666.pdf (accessed June 21, 2017).

Day 23 Evening: From "No Room for Christ in the Inn," December 21, 1862, Metropolitan Tabernacle, Newington, edited by Emmett O'Donnell, http://www.spurgeongems.org/vols7-9/chs485.pdf (accessed June 21, 2017).

Day 24 Morning: From "The Best Christmas Fare," December 24, 1893, Metropolitan Tabernacle, Newington, edited by Emmett O'Donnell, http://www.spurgeongems.org/vols37-39/chs2340.pdf (accessed June 21, 2017).

Day 24 Evening: From "Holy Work for Christmas," December 24, 1865, Metropolitan Tabernacle, Newington, edited by Emmett O'Donnell, http://www.spurgeongems.org/vols10-12/chs666.pdf (accessed June 21, 2017).

Day 25 Morning: From "The Sages, the Star, and the Savior," December 25, 1870, Metropolitan Tabernacle, Newington, edited by Emmett O'Donnell, https://www.spurgeongems.org/vols16-18/chs967.pdf (accessed June 21, 2017).

Day 25 Evening: From "The Sages, the Star, and the Savior," December 25, 1870, Metropolitan Tabernacle, Newington, edited by Emmett O'Donnell, https://www.spurgeongems.org/vols16-18/chs967.pdf (accessed June 21, 2017).

Day 26 Morning: From "Holy Work for Christmas," December 24, 1865, Metropolitan Tabernacle, Newington, edited by Emmett O'Donnell, http://www.spurgeongems.org/vols10-12/chs666.pdf (accessed June 21, 2017).

Day 26 Evening: From "Holy Work for Christmas," December 24, 1865, Metropolitan Tabernacle, Newington, edited by Emmett O'Donnell, http://www.spurgeongems.org/vols10-12/chs666.pdf (accessed June 21, 2017).

Day 27 Morning: From "Going Home—A Christmas Sermon," December 21, 1856, Music Hall, Royal Surrey Gardens, edited by Emmett O'Donnell, http://www.spurgeongems.org/vols1-3/chs109.pdf (accessed June 9, 2017).

Day 27 Evening: From "The Sages, the Star, and the Savior," December 25, 1870, Metropolitan Tabernacle, Newington, edited by Emmett O'Donnell, https://www.spurgeongems.org/vols16-18/chs967.pdf (accessed June 21, 2017).

Day 28 Morning: From "Simeon's Swan Song," January 29, 1893, Metropolitan Tabernacle, Newington, edited by Emmett O'Donnell, http://www.spurgeongems.org/vols37-39/chs2293.pdf (accessed June 21, 2017).

Day 28 Evening: From "He Shall be Great," December 2, 1883, Metropolitan Tabernacle, Newington, edited by Emmett O'Donnell, http://www.spurgeongems.org/vols28-30/chs1760.pdf (accessed June 21, 2017).